# Disruptive Thinking in Our Classrooms

## *Preparing Learners for Their Future*

## Eric Sheninger

ConnectEDD Publishing
Chicago, Illinois

## Praise for *Disruptive Thinking in Our Classrooms*

This book will disrupt your day—it will challenge your thinking, and it will demand reading every page. The nuggets are there: it asks you to adopt business as unusual, the aim is growth, not perfection, and there are no rabbit holes of fluff. Eric Sheninger captures a method for dealing with the unknown, for making the future the present, and invites consideration of the competencies to make learning lovable for teachers and their students.

—John Hattie, Emeritus Laureate Professor, Melbourne Graduate School of Education

This book is an informed reflection from an educator whose experience as a teacher, principal, instructional coach, and persistent learner enables him to affirm the life-shaping potential of teaching even as he chafes in the face of its time-weary practices. Sheninger invites readers to join him in seeking answers to the question, "What makes a classroom become an incubator for student capacity, engagement, and empowerment?" The book reads like a conversation with a worthy colleague as it invites us to reconsider virtually every aspect of teaching. If you have an inkling that getting better at what we do is a non-negotiable for dedicated professionals, join the author as he probes the status quo and provides practical guidance for changing to address the changing needs of the young people in our care.

—Carol Ann Tomlinson, Ed.D., William Clay Parrish, Jr. Professor, University of Virginia

Eric Sheninger will help you shift your own mindset and the mindset of your students with this powerful, practical work.

—Daniel H. Pink, New York Times bestselling author of *WHEN*, *DRIVE*, and *TO SELL IS HUMAN*

A distinctive shift in mindset will be the tipping point in determining whether your school community moves forward into a promising future or slips back into staid and dated approaches to learning. Sheninger does it again. He provides markers, guideposts, and strategies to guide leaders, teachers, parents, and students into what can be a dynamic, productive, and wonderfully disruptive journey.

—Dr. Heidi Hayes Jacobs, Author, Future Forward Curriculum and Systems Designer

Eric has created a fantastic resource for educators ready to take action and empower all learners. *Disruptive Thinking in Our Classrooms* provides stories and examples that illustrate the importance of shifting your mindset towards innovative practices and emphasizes the importance of viewing learning as a process. If you are an educator looking for a guide to help you step out of your comfort zone, this book is for you!

—Monica Burns, Ed.D., author of *Tasks Before Apps* & Founder of *ClassTechTips.com*

Eric Sheninger's new book *Disruptive Thinking in Our Classrooms: Preparing Learners for Their Future* is written to help educators reflect on their practices in order to assist students to think in meaningful ways. He provides practical approaches to enable this to happen in a variety of schools and classrooms.

—Todd Whitaker, Ed.D, Professor of Educational Leadership University of Missouri

Eric Sheninger has written an engaging and multi-faceted book that ends up making the reader "love" disruption! Disruptive thinking turns out to be disruptive doing; it shows us that learning today in the right way is in fact preparing for tomorrow. Using stories, tools, frameworks, case examples, and more, Sheninger takes us through learning journeys and vignettes. The reader can take any of the eight chapters and treat them as intact learning forays into a rich domain. The lessons are rich and rewarding, and indeed "sticky" as one of the chapters is titled. *Disruptive Thinking* is a richly rewarding book that keeps on giving with its simple, practical action guidelines.

—Michael Fullan, Professor Emeritus, Global Director, NPDL.

"In many cases, we teach the way we were taught and lead the way we were led," summarizes Eric Sheninger about the challenges we face today in education. In this book, Eric summarizes the essential shifts in teaching and learning and points out some principles that should continue. While I wish more schools knew the concepts in Chapter 5 on designing effective blended learning environments pre-pandemic, we cannot look back. As educators, we must firmly face future-forward and *Disruptive Thinking in Our Classrooms* is an excellent guidebook to help us do that. As a world-class principal himself, Eric Sheninger is uniquely qualified to write this book. Let's make classrooms better today!

—Vicki Davis, @coolcatteacher and host, *10 Minute Teacher Podcast*

The COVID pandemic was a tipping point around which fundamental aspects of much of society shifted, from home, to the workplace, to schools. To prepare the learners of today for a rapidly evolving world, we need equally big changes to the fundamental structure of schools—from our classrooms to our boardrooms. How do we set out to do that? Eric Sheninger, a widely recognized leader in school reform, guides the way through the changes needed in *Disruptive Thinking in Our Classrooms: Preparing Learners for Their Future*. From shifting mindsets about what classrooms and schools should do to presenting research-based strategies that work, he provides a blueprint for the transformation to better prepare ALL students for their future and not our past.

—Bill Daggett, Ed.D, Founder of the International Center for Leadership in Education (ICLE) and Successful Practice Network

Disrupting education for the sake of our children's success will only work, so long as it doesn't leave a pile of confused and disheartened educators in the wake of that disruption. Sheninger combines years of expertise and hundreds of coaching hours in the pages of *Disruptive Thinking* as a roadmap for creating thoughtful schools that work for both kids and adults. This is an essential text for leaders and teachers alike, who seek to create a bold new world filled with joyful, engaging, and successful learning.

—Weston Kieschnick, Award-Winning Teacher, International
Speaker, and Best-Selling Author

When disruption enters into our lives our first response is to try and find some level of control and normalcy before we move on. However, after a year of disruptions when it comes to race, technology, and politics, we know that we can't control it, but we do need to learn from it. Sheninger helps us understand not only how these disruptions can help us in the future, but also assist us during our complicated present.

—Peter DeWitt, Ed.D., Leadership Coach/Author/Blogger

Sustainable change can only occur when we disrupt the status quo as well as our own thinking. Eric does a wonderful job using actual experiences and observations along with practical examples on how this can be done.

—Ken Shelton, Speaker/Advisor/Consultant

Let's face it, change isn't easy. To future-proof learning for today's students, we must step outside our comfort zones to fundamentally shift traditional structures and pedagogies. In *Disruptive Thinking in Our Classrooms*, Eric Sheninger shares a blueprint for altering mindsets and developing a relevant, personalized culture, while simultaneously outlining practical strategies and supporting examples to make the needed changes happen—right now.

—Thomas C. Murray, Director of Innovation, Future Ready Schools

Eric is considered one of the leading experts in innovative teaching and learning. In this book, he provides practical strategies for educators to help students prepare for an ever-changing world. The stories he shares tug at your heart and the strategies move you to implement them right away in your classroom or school.

—Dwight Carter, educator, speaker, author

*Disruptive Thinking in Our Classrooms* gives readers applicable strategies and resources to meet the needs of learners in 2021 and beyond. This book provides a wealth of ideas for educators to digest and make their own in order to promote the success of students in a remote, hybrid, or traditional setting. Sheninger reminds us once again that people, pedagogy, and technology can be an unstoppable force that moves students from on-task to engaged.

—Brad Currie, NASSP National Assistant Principal of the Year (2017), Founder Partner, *Evolving Educators LLC*

In this immensely practical book, Eric Sheninger takes the reader from the complex challenges of learning at high levels to minute-to-minute engagement in the real world of the classroom. At a time when standardized tests threaten to overwhelm students and teachers, the author makes a compelling case that assessments and, in particular, performance tasks, can be tools for learning—not merely means to rate and evaluate students, teachers, and schools. An especially important contribution is the transformation of the education of the "whole child" into very specific professional practices that teachers can apply on a daily basis in the classroom. Most importantly, at a time when reliance on technology threatens to homogenize learning and standardize education, Sheninger reminds us that personalization—for the student and the teacher—is at the heart of relationship-based learning.

—Douglas Reeves, Author, *Achieving Equity and Excellence* and *Deep Change Leadership*

Mission-driven breakthroughs are borne of disruptive thinking, nurtured by disruptive habits, and strengthened by disruptive action. As we mature during this season of chaos, crisis, and unpredictability, Eric Sheninger's book is a beacon in the fog with an illuminated reminder for us to not return to who we were, but to emerge as the best version of ourselves.

—Ken Williams, Chief Visionary Officer, *Unfold The Soul*

Learning, during recent and uncertain times, has become responsive and fluid, which can be both exciting and overwhelming. Just when we, as educators, think we have a grasp on the "new normal", it changes again. *Disruptive Thinking in Our Classrooms: Preparing Learners for Their Future*, is exactly the book educators need to future-proof their practice. In this book, Eric Sheninger does a masterful job of providing the perfect blueprint and guide to lead education into the future.

> —Laura Fleming, Educator, Author, Founder of *Worlds of Making LLC*

There is no greater disruptive thinker in this world than Eric Sheninger! If we are to truly create cultures of learning and not just teaching in our schools, we must shift our current mindsets and focus on the individual needs of each and every student. In these challenging times, we need strong and passionate leaders who are ready to disrupt the status quo without any fear. In *Disruptive Thinking in Our Classrooms*, Eric has written the manual for leaders like me who want to be more equity-focused and connected in a powerful way to our teachers and students. Read this book twice!

> —Salome Thomas-EL, Ed.D, Award-winning principal, author, and speaker

Disruption? It sounds unpleasant or bothersome. But disruptive thinking is what we need to do to ensure that our students are future-proof. Thankfully, there is a resource that helps us develop the skills necessary to engage in this disruptive thinking and make learning sticky. If you're ready to update your mindset about the future, this book is for you.

> —Douglas Fisher & Nancy Frey, Professors of Educational Leadership, San Diego State University

Eric Sheninger has written yet another book that speaks directly to the current times that we find ourselves in the world in general and in our schools in particular. The concept of "future-proof learning for all kids" completely caught my attention which is essential relative to ensuring that despite the unforeseen challenges of a world that our children will inevitably be confronted by their overall learning experience must sufficiently prepare them to overcome these challenges. I love the book and fully endorse it as a must-read.

—Principal Baruti Kafele, Retired Principal, Education Consultant, Author

Eric does a fantastic job of valuing where schools are, while also challenging them to move forward and become spaces where disrupting thinking is not reserved for pockets of the organization. The stories will make you think, but the challenges will move your practice forward. Packed with resources, *Disruptive Thinking* will help all schools take the next step in providing an environment where the leaders of the future can start leading today.

—Joe Sanfelippo, PhD., Superintendent, Author

A roadmap for a continuously changing world seems impossible, but somehow Eric Sheninger does it with this challenging and extremely helpful book.

—Jim Knight, Senior Partner, Instructional Coaching Group

Eric Sheninger's thoughtful approach to ensuring we are preparing our kids for their future, not our present, is both compelling and needed. Every adult who interacts with children should read and re-read this book. The stories, proven practices, and challenges will push our hearts and minds to think beyond what is and create what is possible in education.

—Deb Delisle, CEO, Alliance for Excellent Education and former Assistant Secretary, US Dept. of Education

This publication is available at discount pricing when purchased in quantity for educational purposes, promotions, or fundraisers. For inquiries and details, contact the publisher at
info@connecteddpublishing.com

Published by ConnectEDD Publishing LLC
Chicago, IL
www.connecteddpublishing.com

Cover Design: Kheila Dunkerly

Disruptive Thinking in Our Classrooms: Preparing Learners for Their Future/
Eric Sheninger. —1st ed.
Paperback ISBN 978-1-7348908-9-1
Ebook ISBN 978-1-7361996-2-6

# Table of Contents

## PART II - Re-Thinking Learning

## PART III - Re-Thinking the Learner

## PART IV - Re-Thinking Our Mindset

# PART 1:

## RE-THINKING "NORMAL"

# CHAPTER 1

# A Bold New World

*"It is what we know already that often prevents us from learning."*
Claude Bernard

One of my favorite shows as a kid was *The Jetsons*. Even though it only aired for one season in the 1960's, I got my fill thanks to non-stop reruns throughout my childhood. For those who have not seen the show, it focuses on a futuristic family residing in Orbit City, whose architecture looks like it was invented by Google with all the living residences and businesses raised on adjustable columns high above the ground. This is where George Jetson lived in the Skypad Apartments with his wife, Jane, and children, Judy and Elroy. There was also a robotic maid called Rosie and their dog, Astro. The entire series revolved around the family's life one hundred years into the future assisted by labor-saving technologies that often broke down in humorous ways.

*The Jetsons* provided us with a glimpse into what society could look like one day and inspired people young and old to dream about the future. Some of the show's bold predictions actually came true, including video conferencing, robots, smart watches, drones, jetpacks, holograms, and automated homes. Other inventions are within our grasp such as flying cars, driverless vehicles, and computers so powerful they have the operating capacity of the human brain. Things are moving fast in our world. In the words of the wise Ferris Bueller, "Life moves pretty fast. If you don't stop and look around once in a while you could miss it." (Hughes, 1986). This is spot-on advice to keep in mind as we enter further into our own *Jetsons* moment.

We live in exciting times despite the fact that it is often difficult to keep up with how fast society is changing. Many of us can remember a world in which there was no Internet and no smartphones. Now we not only have smart watches, but rumors are swirling that a global WiFi network powered by commercial airliners is in the works that will provide people Internet access virtually anywhere in the world. We have seen major disruptions across the service sector. Some of us remember when there was no Uber or Airbnb. Now millions of people are hailing rides and booking rooms in ways that are more convenient and cost-efficient than their traditional counterparts. With the exponential rate of change taking place in society, it is exciting to think about what the future may hold, despite many unknowns. What we do know, however, is the future will be vastly different than what we are currently experiencing and that these changes will dramatically impact workforce expectations.

## The Future of Work

Rampant innovation and exponential advances in technology are changing the societal landscape. Entire industries and professions are being redefined or completely eliminated. Here is a fact: Millions of jobs have been—and will continue to be—lost in the face of numerous disruptive forces that are constantly changing the job market. Technologies might look different, but their disruptive impact will remain the same.

As technological breakthroughs continue to rapidly shift the frontier between the work tasks performed by people and those performed by machines and algorithms, significant transformations in the global job market are likely to continue. These transformations, if managed wisely, will lead to a new age of inspiring work, meaningful jobs, and improved quality of life for all. However, if they are managed poorly, we run the risk of widening competency gaps, increased inequality, and broader polarization. In many ways, the time to shape the future of work will always be the present moment.

Because the world around us is constantly changing, trends become increasingly fickle things; ongoing innovation leads to new processes and pathways on a daily basis. What was trendy yesterday becomes passe today. I don't consider myself a futurist, but I am going to take a stab at making some predictions that will impact the future of work:

1. Automation, robotics, and artificial intelligence will dramatically impact virtually every industry.
2. Job availability will increase amid significant disruptions to the status quo.
3. The division of labor between humans, machines, and algorithms will continue to increase at fast rates.
4. New workplace responsibilities and environments will drive demand for new or refined competencies.
5. Lifelong learning and the ability to think differently will be the keys to both individual and collective success.

There is a great deal to unpack here. To begin, let's focus on the most critical overreaching element. No one can accurately predict the future. As a parent, this terrifies me because both my children will be thrust into this world very soon. There is some good news, however. In the midst of this disruptive change, millions of new jobs will be created. Will our learners be ready? The future of work requires new skills, and it is up to the K-12 education sector to lead the charge in this area. Skills are not enough, in my opinion. Yes, we want learners to possess the requisite knowledge and skills to meet the needs and demands required of them. More importantly, it is our duty and the role of education to ensure they are confident, competent, and contributing members of society. Above all else, our learners must be able to think and learn differently.

Empowering our learners to think critically and solve real-world problems must be a cornerstone of our mission as educators. However, lifelong learning is a must for all of us, not just the kids we serve. For our students to meet the demands and expectations for work now and in the future, *we* must commit to professional growth now and in the future. We must *make* the time to learn and grow as opposed to *finding* the time. If we rely on the latter, chances are it will never happen. Lifelong learning can come in many forms, but in my opinion, the most practical and time-friendly option is the creation and use of a Personal Learning Network (PLN). Using social media allows us real-time access to the most relevant ideas and knowledge that can be immediately implemented into practice to better prepare learners for their future. The time is now to move the needle on transformational change in education. The longer we wait, the greater the risk to those we serve—our kids—and to our future society.

A great deal has been written about the future and the importance of preparing students with the skills, mindset, and attributes necessary for success in a rapidly evolving world. Truth be told, this is quite the harrowing task and one that should compel us all to pause and critically reflect not only on where schools currently are, but more importantly, where our students need them to be. If we continue down the track of sustaining outdated practices in education, we will continue to churn out a population of students who may be good at "doing school," but may not be prepared to do well in life. This applies not only to K-12, but also higher education. Change is not coming; in fact, it is already here, beating down the schoolhouse doors. It's a wake-up call of sorts for educators to think deeply about what we do and how we do it. It is a daunting challenge, yet an exciting opportunity to impact the future.

With the rapid pace of technological change—specifically advances in robotics and artificial intelligence—it is nearly impossible to hypothesize the types of jobs that will be available in the future. Thus, the education profession needs to create a thinking and learning culture that not only inspires students today, but also prepares them for success in their future. This means re-integrating trade-based courses and programs that were the norm in virtually every school not too long ago. After all, the world will still need plumbers, electricians, carpenters, and auto mechanics well into the future. The caveat here, however, is to employ disruptive thinking to create new areas of study and exploration within these traditional areas of content. These revamped programs should afford students the opportunity to use real-world tools to engage in meaningful work that aligns with a future-focused vision. How well schools do this might ultimately determine not only the success of our students, but a prosperous future for society as a whole.

Without a crystal ball, it is difficult to foresee with certainty what the future will hold. However, an endless array of cues garnered from technological innovation affords us the opportunity to reinvent schools in ways that can provide students a fighting chance in a rapidly-changing world. We must first acknowledge the fact that the way many of us were taught and assessed has decreasing value in today's world, let alone the future. The second acknowledgement is that an infatuation with standardized test scores, grades, and homework will only result in schools going deeper down the rabbit hole. Something must give.

The new world of work requires a new way of doing school. A business-as-usual model based on efficiency, repetition, and knowledge acquisition will only prepare students for a world that no longer exists. Competencies that emphasize the unique abilities specific to human beings will enable not only current, but also future generations of learners to prevail in a world where technology will eventually replace most jobs currently available. The challenge for education is to embrace new modes of thinking and innovative practices that are disruptive in nature—and difficult to assess using traditional metrics. This shift will not be easy, but the outcomes we realize will be well worth the investment.

## Disruption is Here to Stay

Education is ripe for disruptive change leading to innovative practices that improve learning outcomes for all students. What might have worked in the past will not necessarily have the same impact today, as the world has changed dramatically in a short period of time. The COVID-19 pandemic provided us with a glaring reminder of the power of disruption. Entrenched traditional practices, the implementation of remote learning with no regard to research or best practices, and the emotional upheaval in the lives of our students caused us to react. We can learn from this experience as well as current and future forces to be proactive going forward. If we don't pay attention and act on lessons learned, we can't move forward. It's safe to say that the seismic shifts we are witnessing as a result of technological advances will continue to reshape our world in ways that we could never have imagined. Disruption has become commonplace in the new world and organizations have moved from adaptation to evolution in order to not only survive, but thrive.

We can learn many lessons from the past about change and disruptive leadership as certain organizations have embraced innovative ideas while changing the way in which they learn. Let's take a walk down memory lane to see firsthand some powerful examples of disruptive innovation in action. Remember the days when many of us had a Blockbuster video card? Without one, you could not rent a VHS tape of your favorite movie. If you did, the joy of watching the latest movie was often squashed upon arrival to the store because all the copies were quickly rented out. This didn't change much when we saw the shift from VHS to DVD. So where is Blockbuster today?

You likely know the answer to this question already and that Netflix largely caused the demise of Blockbuster. Netflix was willing to innovate and change the way they learned. No brick and mortar stores, DVDs by mail, and eventually streaming video. Blockbuster never really knew what hit them until it was too late. The innovative ideas embraced and employed by Netflix were much more consumer friendly. They also aligned nicely with the technological changes that were occurring. The stubbornness and shortsightedness of Blockbuster along with their unwillingness to move away from business as usual resulted in their ultimate demise.

Let's look at another example. How many of us had a Blackberry as our first smartphone? I sure did and many people still make fun of me for it as I held on a bit longer than most. Well, the story of Blackberry ended just about the same way as Blockbuster. Apple and Steve Jobs disrupted the smartphone business with the advent of the iPhone. Not only did the iPhone decimate Blackberry and forever knock it off the pedestal as the gold standard mobile device, but it also sparked the smartphone wars. Virtually every touchscreen smartphone device today has come to us thanks to the iPhone. This is another example of a willingness to innovate coinciding with a fundamental change in how we learn.

Here is one final example that unfolded right before many of our eyes. The taxicab industry was steadfast in its opposition to change. Any attempts to innovate became futile even as Uber descended on an industry that was not very consumer friendly. Uber owns no physical cars, yet is valued in the billions. Anyone can get a vehicle using a consumer-friendly app to hail a ride for a fraction of the cost of a cab. In some cities, you can even order food, helicopters, and jets via such apps. Don't think for a minute that Uber is waiting around for the next disrupter to come along and eliminate their business model. They truly understand the nature of disruptive innovation and change and are committed to staying ahead of the curve. They are currently doing so by investing in driverless cars. Their commitment to embracing innovative ideas and a relentless pursuit of learning will likely keep them relevant in future years.

There are powerful lessons the education profession can learn from the above stories about disruptive innovation. In many ways, I see similarities between our education system and Blockbuster, Blackberry, and the taxicab industry. Even though there have been incremental changes resulting in some isolated pockets of excellence in schools across the world, systemic change remains elusive. By employing disruptive strategies, we can begin the process of creating a more relevant learning culture for our students. If we do not, history has already provided a glimpse as to what might happen.

Disruptive innovation compels educators to go against the flow, challenge the status quo, take on the resistance, and shift our thinking in a more growth-oriented way. If we hang on to the same type of thinking, we will continue to get the same old results—or worse. Now is

> Disrupt the system
> as we know it by
> embracing
> a "business as
> unusual" model.

time to go down the path less traveled and create systems of excellence that will be embraced by our learners and better prepare them for their future. Think differently. Learn differently. Disrupt the system as we know it by embracing a "business as unusual" model. Let's create a new normal.

## A Literate Learner

We are at a crossroads in education. Traditional measures of success often blind us from the truth. Consider looking at the current job market and see where trends reside by conducting an audit. Then compare these to your lessons, curriculum, course offerings, pedagogy, learning spaces, available technology, schedule, and other key components of education to determine how prepared your students are for the current workforce. Take your audit one step further and determine how/ if imagination, negotiating, questioning, empathizing, storytelling, connecting, creativity, and design are emphasized in your classrooms and schools. This audit may surprise you, but will help you determine your preparedness for the new world of work awaiting your students.

The conditions that impact and influence learning have and will continue to evolve. For change to occur, it is essential to continually evaluate where we are at in the learning process to eventually get where we want to be—and where our learners need us to be. Ownership and empowerment result when we create meaningful opportunities for kids to explore, interact, design, and create in real-world contexts. Table 1 below identifies five key *Learner Mindsets* that will help learners prosper now and in the future. Beneath each of the five overarching mindsets are five more specific *Learner Behaviors* our students need to acquire now and continue to refine tomorrow and throughout their learning and living journey. To what extent are we developing the mindsets and behaviors depicted below within our learners?

**Table 1: Enduring Learner Mindsets**

| Ideation | Creativity | Connection | Application | Storytelling |
|---|---|---|---|---|
| Critical Thinking | Unstructured Play | Networking | Entrepreneurship | Emotional Intelligence |
| Reflection | Resilience | Collaboration | Project-Based Learning | Multimedia |
| Cognitive Flexibility | Authentic Exploration | Personalization | Global Awareness | Relational Skills |
| Complex Problem Solving | Growth through Failure | Empathy | Workflow Management | Transparency |
| Analytical and Computational Thinking | Innovation | Communication | Digital Tool Use | Design |

## Belief in a New Way of Thinking

Our beliefs, values, and experiences all work to shape our respective practice. When it comes to learning, the emphasis must be on what *students* do in our schools, not the adults. Therein lies the significant distinction between teaching and learning. It's not that the former is obsolete, but ultimately kids should be more actively engaged than their teachers in the thinking and the work they do. As we strive to create powerful learning opportunities, it is important to reflect upon and update our belief system as needed.

What do you believe in professionally? We all possess a particular set of convictions that are shaped by our respective values system. These impact our work and ultimately determine whether we are successful. Mark Lenz provides this perspective:

*"Beliefs. We all have them. They came from somewhere. They probably started forming in us as young children and have been strengthened through time. Or maybe they've changed over the years. Changing a belief or a belief system is a big deal because our minds are wired to think that our beliefs are the correct ones. It's been said we are creatures of habit. That's because we believe the way we do things, the way we think, is right."* (2016, para. 1)

I would wager that many of our assumptions in education stem from how we were taught throughout our own educational journey. Others were likely adopted based on how we were led or the ways in which teaching, learning, and leading was modeled for us. In either case, once beliefs are established, people have a difficult time changing them when challenged. In order to be our best selves—and best serve our students—what we embrace can and should evolve over time. In a world influenced by disruptive change and in which information is readily accessible, it only makes sense that we adapt what we currently believe or even develop a whole new set of values.

Having a set of beliefs that align with professional values can be a tremendous asset when it comes to creating a vibrant learning culture primed for success. While these are intertwined, there are some important differences. Values are what an organization's culture views as the standard for discerning what is just and good. They are thoroughly embedded and pivotal for acting on a culture's beliefs. Beliefs, on the other hand, are the doctrines or principles that people hold to be true. Mine have certainly shifted over the years and began when I moved from a fixed to a growth mindset. They also changed based on my experiences as a teacher and administrator. Truth be told, they will continue to evolve as a result of my work in schools, current research, and examining evidence showing what actually works amid an ocean of never-ending opinions about what educators should be doing.

There is always a starting point for development. It begins with understanding that all kids can learn. Regardless of zip code or label, every single student who walks into a school is capable of learning. We must be cognizant of the fact that each child is unique and, as such, he or she learns differently. Based on this fact alone,

> All kids have greatness hidden inside them. It is the job of an educator to help find and unleash that greatness.

we must be open to differentiated and personalized pedagogical strategies. All kids have greatness hidden inside them. It is the job of an educator to help find and unleash that greatness.

Without relationships, no significant learning occurs (Comer, 1965). Without trust and empathy, no significant relationships can exist. In simple terms, empathy is the ability to understand and share the feelings of another. Bruna Martinuzzi highlights the following:

+ Empathy is the oil that keeps relationships running smoothly.
+ Empathy is valued currency. It allows us to create bonds of trust, gives us insights into what others may be feeling or thinking, helps us understand how or why others are reacting to situations, and informs our decisions.
+ Tips to become more empathetic include: listening, encouragement, knowing people's names, not interrupting, being cognizant of non-verbal communication, smiling, staying fully present, and using genuine praise.
+ Empathy is an emotional and thinking muscle that becomes stronger the more we use it. (2009, para. 1)

Although foundational to building relationships, empathy is not a typical component of teacher training or coursework in the field of education. It is something that we typically learn from our parents, friends, and colleagues. In my opinion, empathy should become a core component of school curricula and the culture of any organization. Truth be told, this can be a difficult trait for many of us to master. Talking about empathy and demonstrating it are two entirely different concepts. Our mindset and certain pre-dispositions tend to place our own feelings and needs before others. This is not always a negative, but something we must be aware of and open to changing.

It is impossible to know what is going on in the minds of kids. Sometimes things can be so bad, students may either act out or shut down completely. It is important to imagine ourselves in the position of our students. This gives us a better perspective on the challenges and feelings of those we are tasked to serve. Better, more informed decisions can result from "walking in the shoes" of those who will be most impacted by the decisions that we make. In the words of Jackie Gerstein, "All kids have worth. Some, though, want to prove to us that they have none. Our job as caring educators is to prove them wrong." (Gerstein, 2015). When times get tough with kids, try to put yourself in their shoes.

As Theodore Roosevelt once said, "Nobody cares how much you know, until they know how much you care." A culture of excellence is created through relationships built on trust and sustained through empathy. Showing we care can be as simple as listening intently or being non-judgmental when others open up to us about their feelings, concerns, or challenges. Success in a bold new world depends on seeing things in the world around us from the perspective of others.

As you think about your professional role, reflect on how you can be more empathetic towards the people with whom you work and for whom you serve. For some students, the only empathy they might experience occurs within the schoolhouse walls. Regardless of your position, understand that trust and empathy are currencies to be valued above all others. You cannot empower people to think if you have not first built a relationship with them based on trust. Empathy not only builds trust, but creates a culture in which students *want* to learn.

What do you believe in? As you ponder this question, think about how your views either help or hinder the success of learners under your care. Beliefs and values help to not only guide, but also influence, our work. As everything around us evolves, so should our thinking. Being open to this shift will go a long way to growing professionally and creating schools that work better for kids. To create meaningful learning opportunities for students, we must decide what actions to take and what mindsets we may need to shift in order to take them.

We live in a world dominated by exponential change that has and will continue to fundamentally impact all facets of society. Disruption is no longer a buzzword, but a reality. To best prepare our learners to flourish now and in the future, the key is to help develop them into disruptive thinkers who thrive in a disruptive world. If we are to develop students who think disruptively, we must examine and reflect on our current teaching and learning practices. We, too, must become disruptive thinkers, which I define as: *replacing conventional ideas with innovative solutions to authentic problems.*

It's time to challenge the status quo when it comes to teaching and learning in our classrooms. Our learners—and their future in a bold new world—depend on it and on us.

**NOTE:** At the end of Chapters 1-7 of this book, I include a "Disruptive Challenge," designed to do just that: challenge educators to disrupt in some way their current thinking or professional practices.

---

### DISRUPTIVE CHALLENGE #1

Use Table 1 to conduct an audit of your practices to see where there is an opportunity for growth. Circle the top 5 most important Learner Behaviors. Why did you pick those 5? What can you do to push the needle in those areas to prepare learners for a bold new world? Share your implementation ideas and strategies on social media using the #DisruptiveThink hashtag.

---

# CHAPTER 2

# Challenging the
# Status Quo

*"Here's to the crazy ones. The misfits. The rebels. The troublemakers.
The round pegs in the square holes. The ones who see things differently.
They're not fond of rules. And they have no respect for the status quo.
You can quote them, disagree with them, glorify or vilify them. About
the only thing you can't do is ignore them. Because they change things.
They push the human race forward. And while some may see them
as the crazy ones, we see genius. Because the people who are crazy
enough to think they can change the world, are the ones who do."*

Rob Siltanen (as narrated by Steve Jobs in Apple's
"Think Different" ad campaign)

## A Shift in Mindset

For every education professional, adversity is a constant reality: lack
of time, not enough resources, outdated facilities, resistant colleagues,
and a slew of mandates/directives, are but a few obstacles facing us. It
can be difficult at times to envision and implement progressive change
when you feel buried by these challenges. I wish I could tell you that

these daily demands will dissipate in the near future, but that would create false hope. Instead, I will tell you what, in my opinion, is the greatest adversary we as educators face and how to overcome it: our own mindset.

The human brain is wired to keep us safe, and as a result we often become averse to change. The status quo and our personal comfort zones create a perceived safety net that is difficult to relinquish. In many cases, we teach the way we were taught and lead the way we were led; our past experiences often dictate or influence our current professional practice. When this mindset is combined with silos that have been erected to protect ourselves and organizations from external information and new ideas, it becomes clearer as to why transformational change is often just an idea that never gets put into motion.

We should take a critical look at the effect fixed mindsets (assuming our character, intelligence, thinking, and creative ability are static givens which cannot be changed in meaningful ways), can have on creating a thinking and learning culture. Shifting our mindset begins with a renewed focus on our senses. As educators, we must constantly make observations and own what we see. One important reflection point: Is your classroom or school preparing students for life or only to do well in school? Just as important as observing reality is *listening* to, not just *hearing* your stakeholders. When we don't listen, people shut down and withdraw. Saying no or refusing to embrace new ideas has become the safe bet against unwanted risk in a time of disruptive change. However, the unfortunate result can be a dramatic decrease in motivation, enthusiasm, willingness to innovate, and respect for one's ability to create a vibrant thinking culture.

A shift in mindset empowers educators to create change, not merely respond to change. It is this shift that can lay the foundation for transformation. How do we do this? By beginning to challenge the way things are done; by replacing the word "no" with the word "yes"; and by focusing on the "what ifs?" instead of the "yeah, buts." This is where Carol Dweck's (2006) research on growth mindset begins to reap professional rewards. Educators with a growth mindset:

+ Embrace challenges.
+ Persist in the face of setbacks.
+ View effort as the path to mastery.
+ Learn from feedback and criticism.
+ Find lessons and inspiration in the success of others.

When educators adopt a growth mindset, the foundation is set to transform classroom culture. Transformational change is a collaborative responsibility requiring action. Transformational educators consistently make observations, listen intently, leverage a growth mindset, and most importantly, act to improve their classroom, school, or organization. They:

+ Focus on vision and empowerment.
+ Embrace risk to facilitate change.
+ Engage in future-focused problem solving to create learning opportunities.
+ Adapt to new situations effectively.
+ Develop and articulate a vision about the future needs of learners.
+ Work with people in a manner that ignites their passions, talents, and desires to attain a shared vision.

Each day we have the opportunity to improve professional practice, creating a better learning culture for students and educators alike. Think about your own practice and the steps you can take to make transformation a reality instead of an overused buzzword.

## Find Comfort in Growth

Complacency has an insidious ability to inhibit our growth. In our personal lives, we may become complacent when we are happy or content with our status quo. Maybe we don't change our workout routines because we have become accustomed to doing the same thing day in and day out. I know I love using the elliptical for cardio, but rarely use any setting beside manual. Or perhaps our diet doesn't change because we have an affinity for the same types of foods, which may (or may not) be good for us. What we are currently doing may (or may not) be working just fine, but it is difficult to grow and improve when one is complacent. This is why we must be open to finding comfort in disrupting our status quo. Without change, we cannot grow and improve.

Complacency plagues many organizations as well. When we are in a state of relative comfort with our professional practice, it is often difficult to move beyond that zone of stability and dare I say, "easy" sailing. If it isn't broke, why fix it, right? Maybe we aren't pushed to take on new projects or embrace innovative ideas. Or perhaps there is no external accountability pushing us to improve. Herein lies the inherent challenge of confronting the status quo.

There are many lenses through which we can look to gain more context on the impact complacency has on growth and improvement. Take test scores, for example. If a district or school consistently performs at high levels, conventional wisdom might suggest that no significant change is needed. However, just because a school or educator might be "good" at something or "good" today, does not mean that change isn't required in other areas or that change is not required in order to become even better tomorrow. It is also important to realize that someone else can view one's perception of something being good in an entirely different light. Growth in all aspects of a learning culture must become the standard. It begins with getting out of actual and perceived comfort zones to truly start the process of creating, maintaining, and constantly improving a dynamic thinking and learning culture.

Joani Junkala shares some keen insights on the importance of stepping outside our comfort zones:

*Stepping out of our comfort zone requires us to step outside of ourselves. If we are going to strive for progress, whether professionally or personally, we have to get comfortable with the idea of being uncomfortable. This isn't easy for everyone. For someone like me, who is a self-prescribed introvert, this can be difficult. Stepping out of our comfort zone requires extra effort, energy, and sometimes forced experiences. It requires us to set aside our fear and be vulnerable. We have to be willing to try something new, different, difficult, or even something that's never been done before. We have to put ourselves out there—trusting in ourselves and trusting others with our most vulnerable self. It's a frightening thought. What if we get it wrong? What if we look silly? Will it be worth it in the end? Will I stand alone? What if I fail? Oh, but what if I succeed and evolve?* (2018, para. 2)

Change begins with each individual in the organization and spreads from there. Growth and improvement start with honestly assessing our current reality. There is no perfect lesson, project, classroom, school, district, teacher, or administrator. There is, however, the opportunity to get better every day. This is not to say that great things are not happening in education. They most definitely are. My point is that we can never let complacency keep us from continually pursuing a better path, one our learners need us to take. Consider the following questions:

+ Are you comfortable where you are at professionally? Why or why not?
+ Is your school, district, or organization comfortable?
+ Where are opportunities for growth?
+ What will or can you do differently to grow and improve yourself and others?

By consistently reflecting on these questions, we can pave a path of disruptive improvement. However, *questions* merely map out the path ahead; *actions* get you moving down that path and, eventually, where you need to be.

## Making the Ascent

I genuinely believe that most people want to get better in their professional role. Who doesn't want to make a difference in the lives of kids? However, I say *most* because complacency, lack of motivation, or not being passionate about the work cause *some* to settle for "good enough." For many of us, we are continually seeking ways to grow and improve our professional practice. Yet even though the desire is there, and efforts are made, challenges arise. These come in two primary forms: excuses and people. Let me elaborate on both.

People are our greatest asset, and when we invest in them, success is likely. To achieve goals as a system, the support of every individual within the system is crucial. Unfortunately, at times people can also play a role that works counter to what we set out to accomplish either at the individual or organizational level. For reasons that vary, some people are not happy where they are or with the success of others, resulting in concerted efforts to undermine and derail the pursuit of improvement.

It is essential to recognize both subtle and not-so-subtle behaviors exhibited by others as you strive to grow. These might be masked by platitudes that get you to rethink putting in the needed time and effort to improve your craft or to move a culture forward. Be confident in who you are and where you want to go. Don't fall victim to the insecurities, fears, and unhappiness that other people might be grappling with as you work to get better. Even as you strive to learn and improve, a growth-oriented educator also helps others do the same. Obviously, it is important to focus on yourself, but in the end, helping the people we work with grow is just as important as what we do for ourselves. The process of achieving goals is much more fulfilling when it is a collaborative effort.

In the words of Jim Rohn, "Excuses are the nails used to build a house of failure." Now this quote might seem a bit harsh, but viewed with an open mind, you will see that it is quite accurate. In many cases, we believe we can't accomplish a task or implement an idea because of the perception that a challenge is too difficult to overcome, or because the idea might have failed in the past. In either case, our minds start to develop excuses as to why something will not or cannot work. Common impediments include not enough time, lack of funding, or too many initiatives. Guess what? These realities are never going away. Growth will never occur if the will to tackle these, and many other impediments, is not stronger than the voices suggesting it cannot be done. If you value something enough, you will uncover a path forward. If not, you will develop an excuse. The key here is to focus on solutions, not problems, even in the face of difficult challenges.

Change is hard at both the individual and organizational level. Maybe it's not people or excuses that get in your way. Perhaps it is your own mind, which can be the fiercest adversary you face on the path to getting better. Confidence and belief are two of the most powerful

> **If you value something enough, you will uncover a path forward. If not, you will develop an excuse.**

forces that help to keep us focused on achieving goals. Just remember this: You are only limited by the barriers you develop for yourself. If we want kids to think disruptively, then we must do the same.

## Chase Growth, Not Perfection

Perfection is something many people (including many educators) seek. In sports, there are defined scenarios when perfection can be achieved. A pitcher can deliver a perfect game if he or she gives up no hits or walks and the fielders commit no errors. In bowling, a 300-game consisting of all strikes is also a sign of perfection. Outside of sports, it becomes even harder, if not impossible, to achieve perfection.

For the most part, it is a fallacy and it certainly does not exist in education. If we constantly chase or strive for perfection, then we will always be disappointed in our performance. This is not to say that we shouldn't attempt to be our best for those we serve, most notably our learners. However, trying to accomplish the impossible day in and day out is not only unrealistic, but also an unwise use of time and resources.

Others may say you are already good or even great, but both of these vague distinctions are really in the eye of the beholder. A mindset shift is in order that requires us all to re-evaluate how we approach our professional practice. The shift is as simple as it is effective: Chase growth, not perfection. By consistently reflecting on where we are today, we can take steps tomorrow to grow, ultimately leading us to where we want to be and where our learners need us to be. Chasing growth is attainable and leads to daily rewards; chasing perfection only leads to inevitable frustration. There is and always will be room for improvement, no matter your role in education or how well your school performs.

Don't put immense pressure on yourself to be perfect. Not only is this unrealistic, it is also unnecessary. Instead, we need only continuously strive to be the best iteration of ourselves.

## Embracing Change

There are many impediments to the change process. One of the biggest culprits is fear. Many times, this either clouds our judgment or inhibits our motivation to take needed risks to both challenge and upend the status quo. In other cases, we might be afraid of failure. I often reflect upon how, throughout the course of history, many of society's most celebrated success stories went through the heartache and letdown of numerous initial failures. These famous failures have influenced our current lives in countless ways. In their eyes, the act of failing was a catalyst to learn from mistakes and eventually implement ideas or create solutions that have fundamentally changed the world. Henry Ford said it best: "Failure is the opportunity to begin again more intelligently."

There is nothing easy about change. The process is fraught with many obstacles and challenges. One such challenge for many of us is letting go of certain things. Our reluctance or inability to move forward when faced with a decision to stay the course or move into uncharted territory can stop change dead in its tracks before it even has a chance to begin. Typically, there are many factors in play, but three common behaviors that keep many of us stuck in our ways include fear, mental habits, and stubbornness. During different points of my professional career, I had to come to grips with each of these factors and how they were paralyzing my ability to think differently. Once I was able to overcome them, the next step was helping others to do the same.

We are all afraid of something. However, we cannot let fear stop us from improving. Fear of the unknown or failure holds us back from moving forward with change. Zig Ziglar explains that, "F-E-A-R has two meanings: 'Forget Everything and Run' or 'Face Everything and Rise.' The choice is yours" (Ziglar in Garner, 2017). Life is all about choices. We can ill afford to allow fear to hold ourselves and our learners back from all that is possible. It is essential to understand that if we fear the risk, then we will never reap the reward that taking the risk provides. When trying something new or different, chances are good that you will fail. If and when you do, learn from the experience and use the power of reflection to improve your practice. By letting go of some of your fear, you will be surprised at what you can accomplish.

I was never one to embrace the mindset that failing at anything was good for you. For the most part, my educational experiences kept me in a box where success was determined by the destination, not the journey. Grades and test scores were the main indicators of how well I did and, with few exceptions, the learning process focused on a linear path. As I have grown professionally and as a learner, one thing I now believe is that success and learning follow similar paths, which are anything but linear and often a convoluted process. It is important that adults understand this if we are to improve education for students at scale.

Upon entering a comfort zone it is difficult for us to step outside it, no matter how hard we try. When it comes to education, we can see many practices that fall into this category. The toughest adversary that many of us face is our mental blocks. We often think we can't do certain things, or we have been lulled into a sense of complacency. Without opening up the mind to new ideas and new ways of doing things, change will never happen. Think about your mental habits holding you back from implementing innovative change. What do you need to let go of first to improve? How might you help the learners you serve do the same?

The last issue that plagues the change process is good old-fashioned stubbornness. It is a trait that can destroy friendships, marriages, and professional relationships. I don't know why people can be so stubborn, but my thinking is that both fear and mental habits influence stubbornness. What are you holding on to that might not be in the best interests of your students or the people with whom you work? I believe this question can serve as a catalyst for changing certain behaviors that negatively impact not only our practice, but also our professional relationships.

## Failing Forward

In life, there are certain truths. One of these is that to succeed, at times, you must first fail. Obviously, this is not always the case, but if you are like me, success doesn't come easily or on the first try. Learning to ride a bike is one of many great examples. The process begins with training wheels to build up confidence, get a feel for pedaling, and learning how to brake. Watching a child zip around on his or her bike at this stage is exhilarating, yet an anxious experience, because of what comes next. The real challenge begins when the training wheels are removed. Anxiety on the part of the adult sets in while fear and self-doubt creep into the mind of the child. I can vividly remember falling numerous times at this stage of the process. In the end, though, each failure became a building block for eventual success.

The point is that fear of failure should not weigh us down, preventing or obscuring a pathway to success. To this day, our personal and professional lives are fraught with varying degrees of failure. However, I know full well that I would be in a much different place today in both regards if I looked on these experiences as negative and constantly dwelled on them. Sometimes it is hard to get over the hump when we don't believe in our abilities and ideas. In the end, though, it all comes down to mindset and learning from mistakes.

William Arunda sums up the distinct relationship between failure and success:

*"Failure is not a step backward; it's an excellent steppingstone to success. We never learn to move out of our comfort zone if we don't overcome our*

*fear of failure. The most progressive companies deliberately seek employees with track records reflecting both failure and success. That's because someone who survives failure has gained invaluable knowledge and the unstoppable perseverance born from overcoming hardship."* (2015, para. 1)

To eventually succeed, you must accept the possibility that you may first experience failure. We have learned this lesson time and time again from famous failures throughout history. The relationship between the two imparts valuable lessons, which can influence our behavior now and well into the future. Below are some essential learnings related to failure and success:

1. Determination is the fuel. You will get knocked down. The question is, will you get back up? Keep trying until you achieve the result you and others want.
2. Use failure as a valuable form of feedback, which can lead to improvement and ultimate success.
3. Face your fears head-on, tackling inevitable obstacles and challenges that are always part of the equation. Ignoring them or shying away will not make them go away and will inhibit your growth.
4. Mistakes are opportunities to learn. The key is not to make the same mistake twice.
5. Consistent effort makes all the difference.

We can learn much more about the success - failure continuum, of course. After focusing at the individual level, it is essential to look beyond ourselves and towards the bigger picture. Success hinges on viewing change as a process, not an event. When working collaboratively within a change process, failure and success become a shared responsibility where the "downs" are worked through together, and the "ups" are collectively celebrated.

Failing forward is the ability to reflect on unintended negative consequences in pursuit of goals and ultimately, achieving success after learning from these pitfalls. It requires a mindset rooted in determination, self-efficacy, patience, resilience, creativity, big-picture thinking, and accountability. Above all else, you need to believe in yourself and your own unique abilities. When speaking to educators about redefining success and failure, I often point to the acronym that many people now use for the word *FAIL: First Attempt In Learning*. But what does this really look like in the context of transformative learning, innovation, and success? Look no further than famous failures throughout the course of history who persevered after many failed attempts. Although there are numerous examples, one I like to share is the story of Henry Ford. Not only is his story inspiring, but the quote presented previously is one of the most powerful quotes related to learning that I know. He was an amazing entrepreneur who forever changed the transportation industry. Even though he eventually succeeded, Ford first experienced numerous failures. From the lessons he learned after each setback, he was able to continuously fail forward, eventually developing an automobile manufacturing process that was cost efficient, produced reliable vehicles, and paid workers well, all while creating a loyal culture (Ford, 1922).

For Ford, securing the necessary capital to sustain his venture was difficult to attain and in the late 1800s, no one had established a standard business model for the automobile industry. Ford convinced William H. Murphy, a Detroit businessman, to back his automobile production idea. The Detroit Automobile Company resulted from this union, but problems arose shortly after its creation. In 1901, a year and a half after the company began operations, Murphy and the shareholders got restless. Ford wanted to create the perfect automobile design, but the board saw little in the way of results. Soon after, they dissolved the company.

Ford recalibrated his efforts after his first failure. He realized that his previous automobile design depended on serving numerous consumer needs. He convinced Murphy to give him a second chance. However, their second venture, the Henry Ford Company, stumbled from the start. Ford felt that Murphy pressured him to prepare the automobile for production and set unrealistic expectations from the beginning. When Murphy brought in an outside manager to supervise

Ford's process, Ford left the company, and everyone wrote him off. These two failures could have been career-ending, but Ford persevered. Several years after the second parting with Murphy, Ford met Alexander Malcomson, a coal magnate with a risk-taking spirit like Ford. Malcomson gave Ford full control over his production, and the company introduced the Model A in 1904. For Henry Ford, failure did not hinder innovation but served as the impetus to hone his vision for a technology that would ultimately transform the world.

The story of Henry Ford is empowering because he did not let failure inhibit his resolve to succeed. Each failed attempt to revolutionize the automobile industry provided the vital learning lessons he needed to create something amazing through disruptive thinking. The story is the same for virtually every other famous person who did not immediately succeed. You must have a desire to change. Then you must follow through with the process of change, which will not always go the way you would like. Ultimately, we must believe in our abilities to transform ideas into actions that produce a better, more successful result. History has taught us that we should never doubt the difference one person can make with the right attitude and commitment to be the change. Those who fail forward can change the world.

> If it is easy, then it probably isn't learning.

Achieving success is rarely easy. The same goes for learning. If it is easy, then it probably isn't learning. Our learners also need to see the value of failing forward. They need to be empowered to think disruptively. To give students a deeper understanding of concepts through authentic application, creation, and the construction of new knowledge, we need to re-evaluate our current practices. Learning through our mistakes should be an iterative component of this process.

Comfort and fear are intimately connected. They represent zones that many of us fall into and have trouble at times finding a way out of no matter how hard we try. Each works as powerful forces to keep us in respective lanes that are perceived to provide benefits, either individually or at the organizational level. The reality, though, is that these zones hold us, and those we serve, back. For change to become business as usual and something that is pursued when needed, it is crucial that we identify where we are currently, moving forward from there to the next step in the growth process.

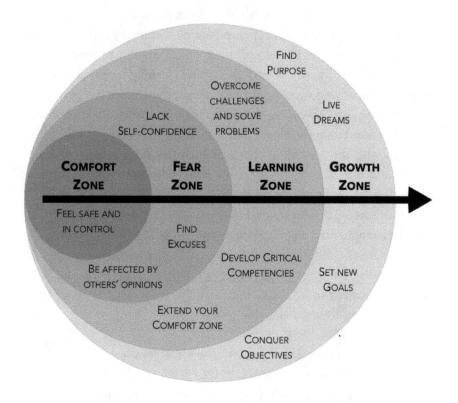

The main idea here is to find comfort in growth. As you look at the elements depicted in the image above, where do you see yourself dedicating the most time and energy? Be careful not to look at these as static zones. There is a great deal of grey in each zone. Consider developing questions aligned to each area, using stems such as why, how, when, and what. Improvement and ultimate success rely on acknowledging the zone where we spend the most time and making consistent efforts to invest more in learning and growth.

## Selfless Acts

One day I headed out to run some errands. It is common practice for me to use this time listening to a variety of radio stations. When I hear any talk between the disc jockeys (are they even still called this?) or commercials, I quickly press the tuning button to get some real music playing. As I fiddled around, I couldn't find anything in particular that piqued my listening interests. After searching and searching, I settled on my favorite Houston station, hoping that when a song began, it would be something I liked.

Since it was a weekday morning, dialogue between the on-air personalities persisted. I was about to change the station yet again, but the story they began to share caught my attention. Firefighters and first responders were sent to the home of a Florida man who had suffered a heart attack while laying new sod on his property. As the man was being treated, he kept carrying on about the fact that he had to finish the job because the grass would quickly dry up and die if it was not installed and watered soon. The firefighters and first responders were like, "Come on, dude, you just had a heart attack. Your life is more important than grass." The man continued to carry on, though, and eventually let it be known why he was so worried about getting the job done. Apparently, he had recently been warned by his local Home Owners Association (HOA) to fix his grass or suffer a fine.

The firefighters and first responders were utterly dumbfounded during this ordeal but patiently worked to treat the man and desperately tried to get him into the ambulance. Still, all he could think about was getting the sod installed and avoiding the fine. Eventually, the man's wife persuaded her husband to get into the ambulance, assuring him that her brother would come over and finish the job. The man who suffered the heart attack was finally on the way to the hospital to get real treatment.

Now comes the good part. After getting the man to the hospital, each firefighter and first responder went back to the man's house and worked side-by-side with the brother-in-law until the job was completed. This selfless act is not only inspirational, but also provides an opportunity for us to reflect on our purpose.

Don't pursue perfection. Pursue growth. One area where there are continuous opportunities for growth is selflessness. It means we act without thinking about how we will profit or be rewarded. If we provide help to others but expect recognition or the favor to be returned, this is not a selfless action. True selflessness means we would perform the deed, even if it were never known to anyone else. Selflessness means we identify with others. Our service to others is not an act of condescending charity; our action is motivated by a feeling of oneness. We help others because we identify with their problems and their suffering. Selflessness is its own reward.

Random acts of kindness always make two people feel better: The person committing the act and the beneficiary of the act. To create a better world for our learners and ourselves, we need to begin by modeling it at the individual level. In the words of Aesop, "No act of kindness, no matter how small, is ever wasted." There is always room for selfless acts in and out of the classroom.

## The Pulse of a Thinking Culture

What makes a successful thinking and learning culture? If you were to ask the majority of stakeholders, they might say that a school or district with high levels of achievement in the form of standardized test scores represents success. Many parents will choose to move to an area and raise their kids there for this reason alone. All one has to do is look at the hoopla surrounding global, national, and state rankings to see that this is often the case. Parents and community members monitor these scores because they have the power to positively or negatively impact real estate values. No matter where your school or district lands in these rankings, there are always disgruntled stakeholders wanting more.

Achievement on standardized assessments is often viewed as the single most important outcome of a thriving learning culture that is preparing students for the demands of their next stage in life, whether grade level promotion or moving onward to college or a career. However, those of us who work in education know this is the furthest thing from the truth. The playing field is not equal in many parts of the world. Privilege is bestowed upon many by the zip code in which they reside or whether a privately-funded education is an option. Thus, in many cases achievement is directly tied to circumstances outside one's control.

It doesn't matter how successful adults think a learning culture is. Quite frankly, it's not about us. We do not work for administrators, central office personnel, superintendents, heads of school, boards of education, or parents. We work for kids. Thus, the best way to get an accurate pulse of a particular learning culture is to engage students as to what they think about the educational experience they receive in school and then see how this compares with traditional metrics. I am not saying test scores and grades don't matter. What I am saying is that the experiences that shape our learners and help them discover their true potential matter more. Some of the best learning that any of us ever experienced wasn't given a grade. It was our ability to work through cognitive struggles, construct new knowledge, and authentically apply what we learned creatively that helped us develop a genuine appreciation for learning.

The bottom line is we need to cultivate competent learners while putting them in a position to see the value of their education. Engaging the number one stakeholder group—our students—in critical conversations about the education they are receiving provides us with an accurate pulse of a learning culture. Just because a student achieves success on a standardized assessment or report card does not automatically imply that he or she appreciates or values the educational experience or will be able to use what has been learned authentically. It also does not necessarily indicate their ability to think in disruptive ways. To determine where your learning culture is, ask students three guiding questions:

+ Why are you learning what you are learning?
+ How will you use what you are learning?
+ What is missing from your learning experience?

It is vital to continually put a critical lens to our work and look beyond what others see as the leading indicator for success. Powerful qualities such as leadership, empathy, integrity, resilience, humility, creativity, and persistence cannot be measured on a standardized test, but they are crucial to future success. A thriving thinking and learning culture blends these elements to not only support the achievement of all learners but also prepare them for their future.

DISRUPTIVE CHALLENGE #2

Engage in a reflective conversation by asking either five students, colleagues, or parents (or all three groups) these two simple, yet revealing, questions: 1. What is one thing about education that should never change and why? 2. What are three things about education that desperately need to change and why? Use the insight you gather to challenge your own mental habits. Share your reflections on social media using either a video or image you create and include the #DisruptiveThink hashtag.

# PART 2:
## RE-THINKING LEARNING

# CHAPTER 3

# Instruction That Works

*"The mediocre teacher tells. The good teacher explains.
The superior teacher demonstrates. The great teacher inspires."*
William Arthur Ward

As I work with more schools in a coaching role, I am beginning to see specific trends emerge. It goes without saying that I see fantastic examples of sound pedagogical practice and innovative strategies that are leading to improved learning outcomes. However, my role, as the schools I partner with and I see it, isn't to just spit out platitudes and tell them what they want to hear. The most important aspect is to empower them to take a critical lens to their work through evidence they collect and begin to think deeply about needed changes to current practices.

It seems like ages ago that I was taking courses to become a teacher at East Stroudsburg University in Pennsylvania. When I think back to my teacher training experience, there were some reasonably consistent areas of emphasis. These included sound classroom management, listing learning objectives, and developing a lesson plan. I still can't believe how much time and focus we devoted to managing a classroom effectively. My professors were proponents of the Instructional Theory Into

Practice Model (ITIP) developed by Madeline Hunter. Thus, once I had a classroom of my own, I implemented what I had been taught to create effective lessons.

For many years this framework was the norm in schools when it came to direct instruction and repetition. The main components are (Hunter, 1967):

+ Stated objectives
+ Anticipatory set
+ Instructional input
+ Modeling
+ Checking for understanding
+ Guided practice
+ Independent practice
+ Closure

Virtually all facets of the ITIP model can still be used in the classroom, although by no means must all steps be part of every lesson.

## What's Old is New Again

Many of the original tenets from this instructional model still have merit today. There is still value in direct instruction. In his meta-analysis of over 800 research studies, John Hattie (2008) found that direct instruction has above average gains when it comes to student results. Another meta-analysis synthesizing over 400 studies indicated strong positive results (Stockard et al., 2018). The effectiveness of this pedagogical technique relies on it being only a small component of a lesson. The rule of thumb during my days as a principal was for teachers to limit any lecture component. Direct Instruction should be designed so that learners can construct (induce) concepts and generalizations. For example, lessons can be divided into short exercises (three to five minutes) on slightly different but related topics. This sustains interest level and facilitates students' synthesizing knowledge from different activities into a larger whole.

We now live and work in different times. Technology, the pursuit of innovation, and advancements in research have fundamentally changed the learning culture in many schools for the better. While conducting thousands of walk-through classroom visits in schools, I am always looking at the convergence of instruction and learning. To me, instruction is what the adult does whereas learning is what the student does. There is some gray area here, but the overall goal is to continually grow by examining current pedagogical practices with the goal of improving learning outcomes for kids. With this being said, I have gone back to the ITIP Model and adapted it a bit. Some items remain, while a few others have been added:

### _Standards-aligned learning target_

These frame the lesson from the students' point of view and are presented as "I can" or "I will" statements. They help kids grasp the lesson's purpose—why it is crucial to learn this concept, on this day, and in this way. Targets help to create an environment in which students exhibit more ownership over their learning. Critical questions framed from the lens of the learner include:

1. Why is this idea, concept, or subject vital for me to learn and understand?
2. How will I show that I have learned, and how well will I have to do it?
3. What will I be able to do when I've finished this lesson?

### _Anticipatory set_

An anticipatory set is used to prepare learners for the instruction or learning to follow. This is achieved by asking a question, adding a relevant context or making statements to pique interest, creating mental images, reviewing information, and initiating the learning process. An intentional "do-now" activity can accomplish this.

The first few minutes of every class are critical to its success, and a pedagogically sound anticipatory set is well worth the time invested when it comes to planning lessons. I get the fact that some educators might question the validity of a strategy that dates back to the 1960s. It is also understandable to have concerns when considering the demands placed on teachers to get through the curriculum so kids are ready for standardized tests. However, creating an anticipatory set need not be labor-intensive.

During some coaching visits to a school district in Mississippi, I was able to observe two great examples. In an elementary classroom as the lesson began, students responded to the following prompt during an English language arts (ELA) block: "If you could be any animal, what would you be and why?" In a middle school classroom, a teacher used a picture prompt, which asked students the following: "What is going on in the picture? What do you see that makes you say that? What more can you find?" In both cases, I observed students writing feverishly because they were driven by interest.

Anticipatory sets should not be a time sap when it comes to planning. Below are just a few quick ideas that can be implemented quickly:

- Picture prompt or memes
- Real-world problem of the day
- Current event or personal story
- Open-ended writing cue that sparks inquiry and creativity
- Riddles
- Short, engaging videos followed by a turn and talk
- Gifs
- Sensory exploration
- Props

Be sure to take advantage of the opening minutes of each class. Starting lessons off with a bang not only makes sense, but also pays dividends in terms of student learning and engagement.

### Review prior learning

A well-structured anticipatory set gets the ball rolling while a review of prior learning immediately after helps to ensure that students understand what was covered previously. Just because something was presented in class, we cannot assume that students actually learned it, which makes reviewing prior learning critical.

Research in cognitive science has shown that eliciting prior understandings is a necessary component of the learning process. Research also has shown that expert learners are much more adept at the transfer of learning than novices and that practice in the transfer of learning is required in good instruction (Bransford, Brown, and Cocking 2000). Consider asking essential questions that were used the previous day.

### Modeling

Modeling is a pedagogical strategy whereby the teacher or student(s), demonstrates how to complete tasks and activities related to the learning target. It describes the process of learning or acquiring new information, skills, or behavior through observation, rather than through trial-and-error attempts or direct experience. Learning, in many cases, results from observation (Holland & Kobasigawa, 1980). Modeling is one of the most effective ways to learn any new skill or knowledge (Bandura, 1986). Showing learners how to solve a problem or tackle a concept is often much more helpful than merely telling them.

### Checking for understanding

Checking for understanding consists of specific points during the lesson or task when the teacher checks to see if students understand the concept or steps and how to enact them to achieve the learning target. It clarifies the purpose of the learning, can be leveraged as a mechanism for feedback, and can provide valuable information used to modify the lesson. Dylan William (2011) poses the following question stressing the importance of checking for understanding while still in the midst of learning:

*"Does the teacher find out whether students have understood something when they [students] are still in the class, when there is time to do something about it?"*

Formative assessment at the end of the lesson is a no-brainer. This can be incorporated as a part of closure, monitoring during collaborative learning time or individual work, independent practice, or through the use of technology. Regardless of the method used, the key is to determine whether learning has occurred by the end of a lesson. I want to focus on some simple and easy-to-implement ideas that can help check for understanding throughout a lesson.

Questions, questions, and more questions are one rule of thumb. Asking, working with, and answering questions is at the heart of facilitating learning. Learning must be an active process. Asking a question is an action. In my role as a coach, I almost always see teachers asking questions. The key, though, is to make sure questions are focused not just on recall of knowledge and facts, but whether kids genuinely understand the concept being addressed. To initiate higher-levels of student thinking, consider how you will integrate the following types of questions in lieu of knowledge-based, recall, or one-word response questioning strategies:

- *Open-ended*: There is no better way to move students beyond stating what they know than getting them to explain their thinking. These types of questions naturally allow for the sharing of more information such as feelings, supporting details, attitudes, and a deeper understanding of the concepts being presented. They require learners to rationalize and reason beyond figuring out the answer by formulating a stance or opinion. Typically, there is no definitive right or wrong response.
- *Evidence-based*: These types of questions empower students to justify their response through rebuttal. The teacher provides both valid and invalid statements seeking responses that are supported with some sort of evidence. The use of evidence allows

students to pull from prior learning while also enabling them to venture deeper into the content.

- *Critical explanation*: Even if a student responds with a correct answer, this questioning technique fosters more critical thought through reasoning. All a teacher needs to do is simply ask "why?" or "how?" to have students probe their thinking a bit deeper.
- *Devil's advocate*: Questions should lead to more questions. This technique pushes the thinking of students by compelling them to consider an opposing view.

Posing verbal questions to students throughout a lesson goes without saying and should be done consistently and intentionally. Teachers should call on both volunteers and non-volunteers when questioning students. In other cases, a few might be selected to go to the board and solve problems while others watch and provide insights. Yet how does one know if each learner in the class actually understands? Below are some easy-to-implement strategies to improve checks for understanding in ways that ensure all kids have the opportunity to respond to verbal questions:

- Provide each student with access to an individual dry-erase whiteboard to respond. You can even purchase clear plastic sleeves or laminate white pieces of copy paper to create extremely cheap options.
- Purchase desks or tables that have a dry-erase surface.
- Lather desks and walls with Idea Paint (ideapaint.com), a low-cost option that transforms any flat surface into a writable space.
- Use available technology tools that are web-based and function as multi-dimensional student-response systems. A list of the latest tools and what they can do can be found at: bit.ly/edtechdisrupt

## *Practice*

Guided practice occurs when students engage in learning target activities under the guidance of a support system that can ensure success.

A common sequence teachers follow is modeling, co-performing the task with students, and then allowing the class to demonstrate learning on their own. Independent practice occurs when learners practice and reinforce what they learn after they are capable of performing the skill without support.

### Authentic application of learning

REAL (relevant, engaging, authentic, lasting) learning in the classroom empowers students to manipulate material to solve problems, answer questions, formulate questions of their own, discuss, explain, debate, or brainstorm. These activities de-emphasize direct instruction and can include discussion questions and group exercises, as well as problem-posing and problem-solving sessions, to get concepts across in a meaningful and memorable way. Pedagogical techniques such as personalized, blended, and project-based learning as well as differentiated instruction and student agency can lead to greater ownership among learners. These will be discussed in Chapter 5.

### Closure

While the opening moments with students are crucial, so are the final minutes. Think about this for a second. What's the point of an objective or learning target, whether stated, on the board, or students having the opportunity to discover for themselves, if there is no opportunity at the end of the lesson to determine if it was achieved? Closure matters, yet many lessons I observe in schools lack this crucial learning component. Learning increases when lessons are concluded in a manner that helps students organize and remember the point of the lesson. Closure draws attention to the end of the lesson, helps students organize their learning, reinforces the significant points of the lesson, allows students to practice what is learned, and provides an opportunity for feedback and review.

Kathy Ganske provides this take on lesson closure:

> "As in a puzzle, an effective lesson has many pieces that must fit
> together. We typically give considerable thought to how we initiate

*lessons: activate or build background knowledge, teach essential vocabulary, engage learners, and set a purpose for the lesson. And we carefully select tasks or activities and texts for use during the lesson. But closure is often given short shrift or omitted entirely. We need to be sure we plan time to cycle back to the what, why, and how of students' learning to help them actively synthesize the parts into a whole. Lesson closure provides space for students to digest and assimilate their learning and to realize why it all matters. Closure is a component of planning and teaching that we can't afford to leave out.* (2017, pg 99)

A Google search will turn up a slew of ideas on how to close lessons. I prefer to keep it simple. First, make sure it is planned for and that at least three to five minutes are set aside at the end of every class. Second, consider the following questions that students should answer or reflect upon in relation to the objective or learning target.

- What exactly did I learn?
- Why did I learn this?
- How will I use what was learned today outside of school, and how does it connect to the real world?

Whether exit tickets, journals, whiteboards, or technology are used doesn't really matter. What does matter is that closure is prioritized as an essential component of learning.

### *Feedback*
Verbal and non-verbal means to justify a grade, establish criteria for improvement, provide motivation for the next assessment, reinforce exemplary work, and act as a catalyst for reflection are all examples of effective feedback. Feedback is valuable when it is received, understood, and acted on (Nicol, 2010). How students analyze, discuss, and act on feedback is as important as the quality of the feedback itself. Make sure it is timely, specific to standard(s) and concept(s), constructive, and

meaningful. Chapter 7 will dive deeper into the importance of feedback in the learning process.

### *Assessment*
Well-designed assessment sets clear expectations, establishes a reasonable workload (one that does not push students into rote reproductive approaches to study), and provides opportunities for students to self-monitor, rehearse, practice, and receive feedback. Assessment is an integral component of a coherent educational experience. For many learners, knowing that they will ultimately be assessed based on the activities and tasks in which they have engaged, increases attentive behavior. A variety of strategies beyond traditional tests can be used, such as performance-based activities, portfolios, and rubrics.

Not all these strategies will be implemented in every lesson, of course. However, each provides a lens for looking at our practices and making needed changes that can lead to better outcomes. It should also be noted that technology represents a natural pedagogical fit that can be used to implement these strategies with enhanced fidelity. Make time to reflect daily on where your students currently are, where they need to ultimately get to, and what the next best steps are for closing that gap.

## The Right Questions

Questioning techniques are an aspect of instructional design that can easily be improved. By looking at question stems, one can determine the level of thinking our learners are expected to demonstrate. Low-level examples almost always begin with who, what, where, or when. These aren't inherently bad, as you need to periodically employ foundational questioning prior to moving up any knowledge taxonomy chart. The problem arises when questioning starts and ends here, without pushing students to apply their thinking in more complex ways. In addition, learners typically find little value or purpose in such questions, beyond merely providing the "right" answer.

Herein lies a major issue with how I see many review games and digital tools used in classrooms today. Typically, they consist of low-level, multiple-choice options. As I mentioned before, there is a time and place for this. However, it goes without saying that an emphasis on recall and memorization will not prepare kids adequately to thrive now or in the future. Disruption caused by exponential change in society and living in a knowledge economy continues to teach us this lesson. If a student can easily "Google" the answer, the question isn't very challenging. Ultimately, questions are more important than answers if authentic learning is the goal.

When it comes to sound questioning techniques, you don't have to reinvent the wheel. Bloom's Taxonomy provides all the guidance any educator needs to determine whether the questions students are being asked empower them to think. The classification system was created by Benjamin Bloom and other educational psychologists in 1956. It represents a hierarchical ordering of cognitive skills that can, among countless other uses, help teachers teach and students learn.

Originally, the six levels of Bloom's Taxonomy, in order (lowest to highest), were: knowledge, comprehension, application, analysis, synthesis and evaluation. All these stages align to cognitive domains, which relate to how the brain processes information and thoughts. During the early 2000's a group of cognitive psychologists provided some minor revisions to the classification structure (Anderson & Krathwohl, 2001). Below is the updated structure:

1. *Remembering* - Recognizing or recalling knowledge from memory. *Remembering* is when memory is used to recall, retrieve, or produce definitions, facts, lists, or to recite previously learned information.
2. *Understanding* - Constructing meaning from different types of functions whether written or graphic messages or activities like interpreting, exemplifying, classifying, summarizing, inferring, comparing, or explaining.

3. *Applying* - Carrying out or using a procedure through executing or implementing. *Applying* relates to or refers to situations where learned material is used through products like models, presentations, interviews, or simulations.

4. *Analyzing* - Breaking materials or concepts into parts, determining how the parts relate to one another or how they interrelate, or how the parts relate to an overall structure or purpose. Mental actions included in this function are differentiating, organizing, and attributing, as well as being able to distinguish between the components or parts. When one is *analyzing*, he/she can illustrate this mental function by creating spreadsheets, surveys, charts, diagrams, or graphic representations.

5. *Evaluating* - Making judgments based on criteria and standards through checking and critiquing. Critiques, recommendations, and reports are some of the products that can be created to demonstrate the processes of evaluation. In the revised taxonomy, *evaluating* comes before creating because it is often a necessary part of the precursory behavior before one creates something.

6. *Creating* - Putting elements together to form a coherent or functional whole; reorganizing elements into a new pattern or structure through generating, planning, or producing. *Creating* requires users to put parts together in a new way, or synthesize parts into something new and different, creating a new form or product.

Educators should develop questions in ways that empower learners to demonstrate high-level thinking as well as mastery of concepts. It is important to note that not every question need be at the uppermost levels of knowledge taxonomy. The key is to try to bump them up when warranted, especially if they are at the foundational knowledge level. If the question stems begin with who, what, where, or when, there is a natural opportunity to tweak them in a way to get to the next level.

Developing and asking thoughtful, intentional questions that engage students in thinking critically is a cornerstone of effective teaching and learning. Even more important, however, is creating performance tasks requiring learners to apply their thinking in relevant ways. This is where the role of instructional design is critical. Challenging learners through an authentic application of what has been learned results in natural inquiry. During numerous coaching visits with schools, I have seen this play out repeatedly. Students are so immersed in an activity that collaboration, creativity, and communication converge with critical thinking spontaneously while they work to solve authentic problems. What results is that students develop and answer their own questions.

## A Framework for Thinking

Studies have shown that students understand and retain knowledge best when they have applied it in a practical, relevant setting. A teacher who relies solely on lecturing does not provide students with optimal learning opportunities. Instead, students go to school to watch the teacher work. The *International Center's Rigor/Relevance Framework*® is a powerful tool that has captured the imagination of educators aspiring to authentically challenge all learners. Educators can use this versatile tool to set their own standards of excellence as well as to plan the learning targets or objectives they wish to achieve.

This framework is a tool to examine curriculum, instruction, and assessment along the two dimensions of higher standards and student achievement. It can be used in the development of both instruction and assessment. In addition, teachers can use it to monitor their own progress in adding rigor and relevance and to select appropriate strategies for differentiation and facilitating learning goals.

The Knowledge Taxonomy (y-axis) is a continuum based on the six levels of Bloom's Taxonomy, which describes the increasingly complex ways in which we think. The low end involves acquiring knowledge and being able to recall or locate that knowledge. Just as a computer completes a word search in a word processing program, a competent person at this level can scan thousands of bits of information in the brain to locate that desired knowledge.

# Rigor/Relevance Framework®

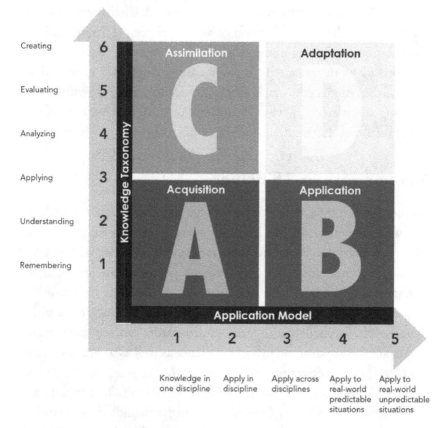

From International Center for Leadership in Education (ICLE). Reprinted with permission. All rights reserved.

The high end of the Knowledge Taxonomy labels more complex ways in which individuals use and develop new knowledge. At this level, it is fully integrated into one's mind, and individuals can do much more than locate information—they can take several pieces of knowledge and combine them in both logical and creative ways. Assimilation is an accurate way to describe this high level of the thinking continuum. It is often a higher order thinking skill; at this level, the student can solve multi-step problems, create unique work, and devise solutions.

The second continuum (*x*-axis)—created by Dr. Bill Daggett—is known as the Application Model. A continuum of action, its five levels describe putting knowledge to use. While the low end of the continuum is knowledge acquired for its own sake, the high end signifies action— use of that knowledge to solve complex, real-world problems and create projects, designs, and other works for use in real-world situations. Each respective quadrant is described below:

A *(acquisition)* - Students gather and store bits of knowledge and information. Students are primarily expected to remember or understand this knowledge. Examples of Quadrant A knowledge are knowing that the world is round and that Shakespeare wrote *Hamlet*.

B *(application)* - Students use acquired knowledge to solve problems, design solutions, and complete work. The highest level of application is to apply knowledge to new and unpredictable situations. An example would include knowing how to use math skills to make purchases and count change.

C *(assimilation)* - Students extend and refine their acquired knowledge to be able to use that knowledge automatically and routinely to analyze problems and create solutions. Here, students embrace higher levels of knowledge, such as knowing how a nation's political system works and analyzing the benefits and challenges of the cultural diversity of this nation versus other nations.

D *(adaptation)* - Students have the competence to think in complex ways. An example would include the ability to access information in wide-area network systems and the ability to gather knowledge from a variety of sources to solve a complex problem in the workplace.

With its simple, straightforward structure, the framework can serve as a bridge between instruction and learning. It offers a common language with which to express the notion of a more rigorous and relevant curriculum and encompasses much of what the world now requires of learners. The framework is versatile; it can be used in the development of instruction, pedagogical strategies, and assessment. Likewise, teachers can measure their progress in adding rigor and relevance to instruction and select appropriate strategies to meet learner needs and higher achievement goals.

## The Meaning of Words

Jargon in education is nothing new. The key is to make sense of such words as they apply to our professional practice. Whether it is in person at events and workshops or in social media spaces, I routinely see conversations play out during which educators take a certain stance on the meaning of specific words. I notice a great deal of time and energy spent on debating the negative aspects of certain words that other educators value.

For example, words such as grit, innovation, branding, mindset, future ready, deeper learning, and personalization come to mind as a few that provoke heated discussion among some educators. Each day, various people chime in stating their critique of such words when an article focusing on its merits arise. Does the meaning in someone's opinion really matter or is it more about the outcome? The important point is the impact the practice and related strategies related to the term have on improving the learning culture of our schools. Do our students feel the same way about these words as the adults who spend energy discounting them? Maybe I am off base with my thinking here, but I try to find value in many of the words listed above because I can see how they contribute to a positive school culture.

One word in particular worth discussing is "rigor." I have seen many people I respect get pretty fired up about the term. Taken out of an educational context, the word rigor can imply being rigid, inflexible, strict, unyielding, tough, or demanding. When considered in these terms, it is no wonder many people take issue with the word. However, I see "rigor" differently and try to share my view when working with other educators.

I view it as a way of framing lessons and learning outcomes at the high end of a knowledge taxonomy. Rigorous learning empowers students to develop the competence to think in complex ways and sets the stage for them to apply their knowledge and skills through relevant means. Even when confronted with perplexing unknowns, students are able to use extensive knowledge and skills to create solutions and take action that further develops their skills and knowledge. This is my view of rigor, including what it is and is not:

**Rigor**: An assignment that challenges students to use critical thinking skills or a learning environment that is challenging, but supportive and engaging.

Rigorous lessons and learning activities ask students to compose, create, design, invent, predict, research, summarize, defend, compare, and justify to demonstrate conceptual mastery and standards attainment. Rigor is quite simply engaging in high levels of thinking, including:

- Scaffolding for thinking
- Planning for thinking
- Assessing thinking
- Recognizing the level of thinking students demonstrate
- Managing the teaching/learning level for the desired thinking level

**Rigor is NOT**:

- More or harder worksheets
- AP, gifted, or honors courses
- The higher-level book in reading

- Covering more content
- More homework

Rigorous learning is for all students. The perception that rigor applies only to a certain group is near-sighted at best and damaging to learners at worst. Herein lies another point of confusion with the word. All students not only deserve rigorous learning expectations, but should also be made to feel that they can handle these higher expectations.

Not being flexible with the meaning of educational words and terms seems to be a bit hypocritical. Taking the opposing side of terms that others find useful in itself seems a bit rigid, strict, and unyielding. Words in education are what you make of them. Try to have an open-mind and the inherent value of such words might provide more context for your own work and goals, but more importantly, that of your students.

## Making Connections

One afternoon I was working from home, which was a rarity for me prior to the pandemic. I huddled in my home office and focused my attention on responding to emails, writing a blog post, tweaking some presentations, and updating the digital handouts that all participants receive during one of my keynotes or workshops. Always joining me on these work-from-home days are my beloved dogs Roxie and Taz. As usual, they were perched atop the couch, asleep. Roxie's snoring not only brought a smile to my face but also made me jealous that she doesn't have a care in the world and enjoys the life of a pampered pet.

Later in the day, I moved from my desk and joined the dogs on the couch. Before I knew it, I apparently dozed off. I realized I had fallen asleep when my son, Nick, awakened me as he returned home from school. Now, I was enjoying one of those deep-sleep naps, so I was a tad bit annoyed that he interrupted this moment of pure bliss. My annoyance with him was short lived, however, when I learned he had woken me up to share a current project he completed in school.

My 7th-grade son at the time stood above me holding a bridge he had built as part of an engineering project. As he provided details on how he went about constructing it, I could see how proud he was of his creation. Nick was beaming as he informed me that his bridge ranked 5th best out of a class of 28 students. Usually, it is my daughter who comes home from school and consistently engages my wife and me in conversations about how awesome her day of learning was. This was not typically the case with my son, so I relished the opportunity to dive more deeply into his learning experiences in this particular class.

My son was fortunate to have engineering every day as a 7th grader. Throughout the year he brought home innovative projects that he created, and each sparked a conversation about why this type of learning was important and how it would benefit him in the real world. The result of these discussions illustrates how impactful the daily experiences were for him. He had been empowered to own his learning by actively applying what he learned in this class while making connections to math, history, and science. Conceptual mastery translated into what he had been able to effectively build with his hands. There were also language arts connections, as students were encouraged to write and speak about the engineering principles behind their designs.

My son became an empowered learner in engineering because many elements were bridged together to facilitate REAL (relevant, engaging, authentic, lasting) learning. Pulling from my son's experience, as well as what we know about sound pedagogy, I was reminded that the following elements work together to empower learners:

+ Interdisciplinary connections
+ Authentic contexts
+ Choice
+ Practical application
+ Creation of a product that demonstrates conceptual mastery
+ Meaningful feedback

To prepare students for the world of tomorrow, we must transform

their learning today. The shift is not
as difficult as one might surmise. As
you think about developing or evaluating lessons, learning activities,
projects, and performance tasks, ask
yourself if the six elements above are
integrated. If they are, then chances
are that your students will not only
be empowered but also develop

> To prepare students
> for the world of
> tomorrow, we must
> transform their
> learning today.

a greater appreciation for learning. Happy learners are empowered
learners when the right connections and elements are bridged together.
What results is the foundation for disruptive thinking.

## Relevance Drives Thinking

There are many important questions that we must ask and attempt
to answer if we want to produce students who are actively engaged in
thinking and learning. Many of these questions start with what or how.
Simon Sinek (2009) reminds us that the most important questions we
should be asking begin with a focus on why.

His idea brings some needed context that can help to drive meaningful change in any organization. For the most part, every organization knows *what* they do. Some organizations know *how* they do it.
However, as Sinek goes on to explain, very few organizations know *why*
they do what they do. Now substitute organization with classroom.
The why centers on purpose, values, belief, and feelings. The what, and
to a certain extent the how, have a certain amount of clarity around
them. The why is a totally different animal and always a bit vague in
many classrooms. It is difficult to articulate at times; thus, we take the
path of least resistance and focus our questions and efforts on the what
and the how.

The why matters more than ever in the context of schools and
education. Step into the shoes of a student for a moment. If he or she
does not truly understand why they are learning what is being taught,

the chances of that student becoming highly engaged and empowered to think critically diminish significantly. Each lesson should squarely address the why behind the intended learning outcomes. What and how we assess carries little to no weight in the eyes of our students if they don't understand and appreciate the value of the learning experience.

A focus on the why is a good start, but holding ourselves accountable is another story. Therefore, as principal I asked teachers to include an authentic context and interdisciplinary connections into every lesson and project they designed and implemented with their students. We ensured accountability through numerous observations, walkthroughs, collection of artifacts, and adding a portfolio component to the evaluation process. Unearthing the why became ingrained in the very DNA of our school culture. Relevance should be a non-negotiable in any learning task. If a student does not know why he or she is learning something, that is on us. Learning today and beyond must be personal for every student.

Our work does not stop here. In the larger picture, students also need better responses to the question about why they need school and education at all. Students need to understand why success in school functions to serve them both inside and outside the classroom. A renewed focus on creating schools that work for kids through uncommon learning strategies that are not being implemented in schools at scale can help to transform numerous facets of traditional schooling (Sheninger, 2015). Transforming learning is a momentous task that must be driven by unearthing the why across all facets of school culture.

This conversation around "why" should also translate to professional educators. It is critical that they can articulate the why related to their own work. Take technology, for example. For many educators, simply using technology in their lessons periodically is their sole focus. Some questions I commonly run across include: What are the latest apps and tools I can use in my classroom or school? How can I integrate technology to improve learning? These questions aren't necessarily irrelevant, but they often focus on which tools are used in a lesson, not the learning that must occur in and after the lesson. Just look around at the sessions at many technology conferences. When sessions like "50 Apps in 50 minutes" have standing-room-only crowds, while sessions on "Improving Your Instructional Practices" have far fewer, it is a sign that we are more focused on the *what* and *how* as opposed to the *why* of what we do.

Whether it comes down to effectively using technology, growing professionally, innovating, or improving instruction, Sinek reminds us to always focus on the why first. This allows us to bring clarity to our ideas, align pertinent research, and identify practices in action for further support to instill a sense of value in the work at hand. Students must believe in their school and the value of learning. Educators must believe in the mission, vision, values, and goals of a school to improve. They must also believe in the pursuit of better ways to grow that move beyond sound bites, flashy tools, and ideas with little substance. Unearthing the why behind our work is the key to sustainable change and transforming practice that empowers all learners to think disruptively.

In a nutshell, relevance provides learners with the purpose for their learning. If it is absent from any activity or lesson, many students will be less motivated to learn to their fullest potential. Research on the underlying elements that drive student motivation validates how essential it is to establish relevant contexts. Kember et al. (2008) conducted a study in which thirty-six students were interviewed about aspects of the teaching and learning environment that motivated or demotivated their learning. They found that one of the most important means of motivating student learning was to establish relevance. It was a critical factor in providing a learning context in which students construct their understanding of the course material. The interviewees found that teaching abstract theory alone was demotivating. Relevance could be established through showing how theory can be applied in practice, creating relevance to local cases, relating the material to everyday applications, or finding applications in current newsworthy issues.

Getting kids to think is laudable, yet if they fail to truly understand how this thinking will help them, do they truly value learning?

The obvious answer is no. However, not much legwork is needed to add meaning to any lesson, project, or assignment. Relevance begins with students acquiring knowledge and applying it to multiple disciplines to see how it connects to the bigger picture. It becomes even more embedded in the learning process when students apply what has been learned to real-world predictable and unpredictable situations, resulting in the construction of new knowledge. Thus, a relevant lesson or task empowers learners to use their knowledge to tackle real-world problems that have more than one solution.

> A relevant lesson or task empowers learners to use their knowledge to tackle real-world problems that have more than one solution.

Learners respond well to relevant and contextual learning activities. This improves memory, both short-term and long-term. Sara Briggs sums it up:

> "Research shows that relevant learning means effective learning and that alone should be enough to get us rethinking our lesson plans (and school culture for that matter). The old drill-and-kill method is neurologically useless, as it turns out. Relevant, meaningful activities that both engage students emotionally and connect with what they already know are what help build neural connections and long-term memory storage. In the words of Will Durant based on Aristotle's work, 'We are what we repeatedly do. Excellence, then, is not an act, but a habit.' The point here is that consistent efforts must be made to integrate interdisciplinary connections and authentic contexts to impart value to our learners. Relevance must be student based: the student's life, the student's family, and friends, the student's community, the world today, current events, etc." (2014, para. 2)

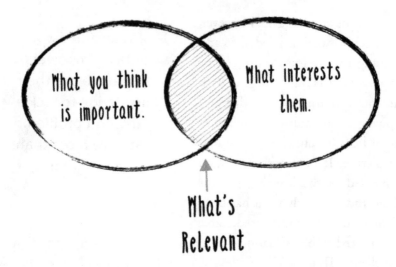

If a lesson or project is relevant, students will be able to tell you:

1. What they learned
2. Why they learned it
3. How they will use the learning (in a meaningful context both in and out of school)

Without relevance, learning will not always make sense to students. We must plan intentionally to ensure that relevance becomes a mainstay in our daily pedagogical planning and practices.

## Content Has Its Purpose

When I think back to my days as a student, the course content seemed to be at the forefront of every class. Whether it was disseminated during a lecture in college, through direct instruction in K-12, or at times consumed from a textbook or encyclopedia, content was everywhere. The more I think about it; content was the predominant focus in every class I ever had. Day in and day out a repetitive cycle ensued in most classes where my classmates and I were given information and then tasked with demonstrating what we learned, or in a few cases, constructing new knowledge. The bottom line is that I, like many other students at the time, "did school" as best we could, never really questioning the process. In the end, for us it was simply about passing the test.

Now, I am not saying that content is not valuable or not needed as a basis to move from low- to high-level learning. It goes without saying that a certain amount of foundational content is required for all of us, such as learning letters and numbers, before moving on to different levels of knowledge construction in language arts and mathematics respectively. But let's face it, as learners progress through the system, delivering content and acquiring knowledge can be easily accessed using a variety of mobile devices. This then begs the question: How relevant is content in a world that continues to evolve exponentially thanks to advances in technology?

When reflecting on this, I think about the following quote from Steve Revington (2016), "Content without purpose is only trivia." Learners today are not always as compliant or conforming as many of us were back in the day—nor should they be.

A lesson, project, or activity that is relevant and has purpose allows learners to use both the content and their knowledge to tackle real-world problems that have more than one solution. An important shift here is key: engaged learning empowers kids to put knowledge to use, not just acquire knowledge for its own sake. Many yearn for and deserve to use content and acquired knowledge in authentic ways. The value in it relies on how it is applied to further develop thinking in a purposeful way.

Being a whiz at trivia might help a contestant on the game show *Jeopardy* but has little value in the game of life. The stakes are much higher now, which means we must consistently analyze our work to continually grow and improve. Helping our learners find greater purpose in what they learn today will benefit them well into their future.

## Bring the Awe

Awe might seem like just another three-letter word, but it is so much more. Humans can get goosebumps when we experience awe, that exuberant feeling of being in the presence of something vast that transcends our understanding of the world. It is a catalyst that can motivate people to do more good. Awe helps bind us to others, motivating us to act in collaborative ways that enable strong groups and cohesive communities.

Go back to the last time you experienced a moment of awe and think about how this impacted you. I would wager that many specific experiences come to mind. Descriptors such as awesome, jaw dropping, satisfying, and rapturous probably come to mind. The power of awe cannot be overstated. When we experience the sensation of awe, we are consumed by wonder, relevancy, emotion, engagement, inspiration, and real-world connections. It is a pivotal ingredient in making ideas resonate.

Various research studies support the many benefits of having our minds stretched in healthy but powerful ways. Researchers from Stanford and the University of Minnesota found that participants who experienced awe, relative to other emotions, felt they had more time available, were less impatient, were more willing to volunteer their time to help others, and more strongly preferred experiences over material goods (Bosler, 2013). Awe is an experience of such perceptual expansion that you need new mental maps to deal with its incomprehensibility.

Applying this concept to education is both exciting and challenging. Awe is a driving force for learning that will not just benefit our students now, but also well into their future. However, traditional views and functions of school deprive certain students from experiencing the joy and power of awe as a catalyst for meaningful learning. Current policies in some schools focus on control, compliance, conformity, and rules that don't exactly inspire awe within our learners. We hear it over and over again—students are disengaged, bored, and disempowered. Systemic change is needed even in schools where there are isolated pockets of excellence, because all students should be exposed to the power of awe.

We have a responsibility to not only teach, but inspire, our students with awe woven into their daily learning experiences. To do this, we must innovate our current practice. In my definition, "innovation" includes creating, implementing, and sustaining transformative ideas that instill awe to improve learning. Increases in our willingness to innovate can result in disruptive changes to thinking and learning.

Disruption in a way that facilitates improved learning opportunities that engage and empower students through awe should be a primary goal of education and educators. In order to drive innovation, there must be a focus on unique learner needs, new technologies, evolving learning environments, and bold ideas.

Schools and educators can take advantage of inherent stimuli in these drivers to create better, more meaningful learning experiences for students that leverage the power of awe. Building off a sound pedagogical foundation rooted in rigor, relevance, and relationships, the drivers of innovation can bring awe back into learning. Let's look at these drivers in a bit more detail:

- **New and Improved Technologies** – Technology continues to change at a rapid pace, which presents education with some exciting opportunities to awe learners. Some examples include augmented reality, virtual reality, open education resources (OER), adaptive tools, coding, drones/robotics, artificial intelligence, holograms, and gamification. With all the excitement and possibilities, it is important to remember that pedagogy trumps technology if the goal is meaningful student learning.
- **Evolving Learning Environments** – You can have all the best digital learning tools and techniques, but if the learning environment remains unchanged, the results that we yearn for might never materialize. Learner-designed spaces, both physical and virtual, emphasize comfort, flexibility, choice, and the use of authentic tools. They are reflective of the real world, leverage the outdoors, and capitalize on technology.
- **Unique Learner Needs** – Learners crave a greater purpose and sense of relevance in their learning. We must seize on the gift that access to real-time information sources provide to foster

student learning anytime, anywhere, and with anyone. Awe can be cultivated in both personal and personalized learning opportunities in which the primary motivation for learning comes from student agency. This culminates in a shift from consumption to creation and curating as a means for students to awe us in their learning experiences.

+ **Bold Ideas** – We must shift from "business as usual" to "business as unusual." Bold ideas work to counteract the status quo and current education reform policies. We must work to elevate the profession, integrate more play into the school day, embrace failure as a natural part of the learning process throughout the system, redefine success and learning, look to either refine or eliminate outdated practices, and provide meaningful professional development with accountability for growth and improvement.

To inspire students, we must make a concerted effort to bring the awe back into learning. This is not an easy journey, but one that is well worth the effort.

## The Role of Technology

Technology has the ability to support and enhance disruptive thinking in the classroom. When implementing any digital tool or initiative, it is imperative not to allow the device to drive instruction. Lessons, curriculum, assessments, and schools should never be built around technology. Everything we do in education should be built around learning. Thus, if the ultimate goal is to improve student outcomes, then the role of technology should be to support or enhance teaching and learning. When it comes to educational technology, sound pedagogy seems secondary at times. Including technology merely for the sake of "using" it as part of a lesson equates to a missed opportunity. If the goal is deep and meaningful learning, we should ensure any digital aspect aligns accordingly.

Most students know how to use technology. However, we cannot assume that they know how to use it to support their learning. This is where attention to sound instructional design is necessary. The key is to determine what we want our students to know, and then let them have a choice as to how they will demonstrate or apply their learning using disruptive thinking. This not only adds authenticity, but also takes the pressure off educators from having to learn how to use an endless number of tools.

It is crucial to maintain a concerted focus on outcomes, construction of new knowledge leading to authentic application, and the development or enhancement of essential competencies. The assessment and feedback pieces are also critical. Digital learning represents a huge investment in time, money, and other resources. With so much at stake, the goal should be placing a powerful learning tool in the hands of our students—not a digital pacifier. Purposeful use can innovate assessment, transform time frames around learning, increase collaboration, allow access to information at any time, and provide a level of student ownership like never before. These are all outcomes that any educator would (or should) openly embrace.

Increasing engagement is a typical motivator for technology use in the classroom, but if that engagement does not lead to evidence of learning then what's the point? Using it simply to access "stuff" is also not a sound use. As educators, it is important to be intentional when it comes to digital learning. If the norm is surface-level integration that asks students to demonstrate knowledge and comprehension, the most beneficial aspects of digital learning are missed.

The question about effective use provides a great opportunity for all of us to critically reflect upon the current role technology plays in education. There is a great deal of potential in the numerous tools now available, but we must be mindful of how they are being used. Take *Kahoot* for example, or any game-based response tool. This is used in many classrooms to get students more engaged and add a level of fun and excitement to the learning process. However, most of the time the questions that students are asked in a *Kahoot* activity are focused on the lowest cognitive domains and mostly multiple choice. I have nothing against *Kahoot* and think it is a tool that has a great deal of promise. My issue is *how* this tool, and many others, are used in the classroom.

The burden of responsibility here lies within each of us. In many cases, the engagement factor is emphasized over learning outcomes and actual evidence of improvement aligned to standards. It should go without saying that effective technology integration informs instruction and provides feedback as to the level of disruptive thinking students demonstrate. Be wary of putting the cart before the horse when acquiring technology and getting it into lessons takes precedence over improving instructional design. In either case, for technology to ever live up to the lofty expectations that have been established, we must take a more critical look at pedagogy. The image below provides a great reference point for ensuring that learners are empowered to think disruptively.

The overall goal when integrating technology should be to provide new and better opportunities for students to work and think. Here is a great guiding question: How are students empowered to learn with technology in ways that they couldn't without it? It is really about how students use tools to create artifacts of learning that demonstrate disruption. What might this look like, you ask? Give kids challenging problems to solve that have more than one right answer and let them use technology to show that they understand. When doing so, let them select the right tool for the task at hand.

Learning is more durable and lasting when students are cognitively engaged in the learning process. Long-term retention, understanding, and transfer are the result of mental work on the part of learners who are engaged in active sense-making and knowledge construction. Accordingly, learning environments are most effective when they elicit effortful cognitive processing from learners and guide them in constructing meaningful relationships between ideas rather than encouraging passive recording of information (deWinstanley & Bjork, 2002; Clark & Mayer, 2008; Mayer, 2011). Researchers have consistently found that higher student achievement and engagement are associated with instructional methods involving active learning techniques (Freeman et

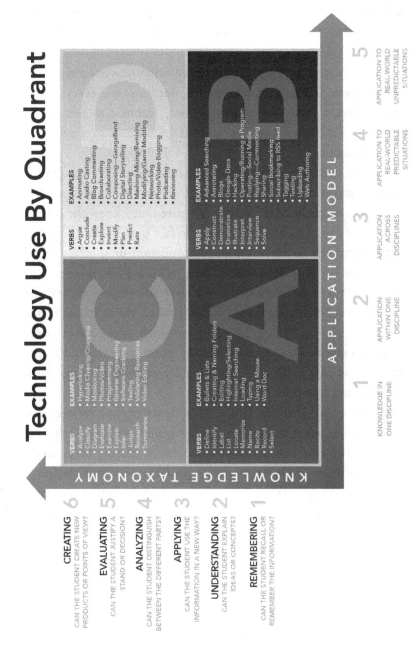

# Technology Use By Quadrant

**KNOWLEDGE TAXONOMY**

**6 CREATING**
CAN THE STUDENT CREATE NEW PRODUCTS OR POINTS OF VIEW?

**5 EVALUATING**
CAN THE STUDENT JUSTIFY A STAND OR DECISION?

**4 ANALYZING**
CAN THE STUDENT DISTINGUISH BETWEEN THE DIFFERENT PARTS?

**3 APPLYING**
CAN THE STUDENT USE THE INFORMATION IN A NEW WAY?

**2 UNDERSTANDING**
CAN THE STUDENT EXPLAIN IDEAS OR CONCEPTS?

**1 REMEMBERING**
CAN THE STUDENT RECALL OR REMEMBER THE INFORMATION?

**Quadrant C**

VERBS
- Analyze
- Classify
- Diagram
- Evaluate
- Examine
- Explain
- Infer
- Judge
- Research
- Summarize

EXAMPLES
- Hyperlinking
- Media Clipping/Cropping
- Monitoring
- Photos/Video
- Programming
- Reverse Engineering
- Software Cracking
- Testing
- Validating Resources
- Video Editing

**Quadrant D**

VERBS
- Argue
- Conclude
- Create
- Explore
- Invent
- Modify
- Plan
- Predict
- Rate

EXAMPLES
- Animating
- Audio Casting
- Blog Commenting
- Broadcasting
- Collaborating
- Composing—GarageBand
- Digital Storytelling
- Directing
- Mashing-Mixing/Remixing
- Modifying/Game Modding
- Networking
- Photo/Video Bogging
- Podcasting
- Reviewing

**Quadrant A**

VERBS
- Define
- Identify
- Label
- List
- Locate
- Memorize
- Name
- Recite
- Record
- Select

EXAMPLES
- Bullets & Lists
- Creating & Naming Folders
- Editing
- Highlighting/Selecting
- Internet Searching
- Loading
- Typing
- Using a Mouse
- Word Doc

**Quadrant B**

VERBS
- Apply
- Construct
- Demonstrate
- Dramatize
- Illustrate
- Interpret
- Interview
- Sequence
- Solve

EXAMPLES
- Advanced Searching
- Annotating
- Blogs
- Google Docs
- Hacking
- Operating/Running a Program
- Posting—Social Media
- Replying—Commenting
- Sharing
- Social Bookmarking
- Subscribing to RSS feed
- Tagging
- Texting
- Uploading
- Web Authoring

**APPLICATION MODEL**

**1** KNOWLEDGE IN ONE DISCIPLINE

**2** APPLICATION WITHIN ONE DISCIPLINE

**3** APPLICATION ACROSS DISCIPLINES

**4** APPLICATION TO REAL-WORLD PREDICTABLE SITUATIONS

**5** APPLICATION TO REAL-WORLD UNPREDICTABLE SITUATIONS

67

al., 2004 and McDermott et al., 2014). When looking at the research, the main takeaway is that student learning success depends much less on what *instructors do* than what *they ask their students to do* (Halpern & Hakel, 2003).

Another key strategy for successful integration is to use technology only when appropriate. Technology will not improve every lesson or project, thus a focus on pedagogy first, technology second—if appropriate—is the way to go. Let's look at an example in the form of digitized discussion.

I wasn't an overly confident student when it came to engaging in open conversations during class. If one of my teachers posed a question, I only raised my hand if I was 99.9% sure that I knew the correct answer. I guess you can chalk this up to the fact that I lacked a certain degree of confidence in my knowledge acquisition or the fact that I was a relatively shy student when it came to class participation. Perhaps it was a combination of both. There were other issues at play that impacted my level of engagement. Not only was I averse to answering questions, but I also rarely directed any to my teachers outside of a one-on-one conversation. Discussions with my peers were limited to the rare occasion when a cooperative learning activity was planned. Such was life in a classroom back in the day.

I often reflect on what my learning experience might have been like if my teachers had access to and used the many interactive tools that are available today to enhance classroom discussion. During every single workshop I facilitate, I have participants in both peer and randomly selected groups engage in face-to-face conversations on numerous question prompts. It is during this time that they get to share their ideas on the topic, discuss implementation strategies, reflect on what others have said, or provide positive reinforcement. I am always inspired when I eavesdrop on these conversations. There is no substitute for real human interaction, as this is the ultimate relationship builder. After a set amount of time, they are then asked to share their responses using one of many different digital tools.

Let me take a step back now and share some insights on why classroom discussion is so meaningful. Todd Finley (2013) shared the following:

*Quality discussion involves purposeful questions prepared in advance, assessment, and starting points for further conversations. Teachers are also advised to:*

- *Distribute opportunities to talk*
- *Allow discussants to see each other physically*
- *Ask questions that may or may not have a known or even a single correct answer*
- *Foster learners talking to peers*
- *Encourage students to justify their responses*
- *Vary the types of questions (para. 3)*

Research supports the importance of discussion when backed by the purposeful use of technology. Smith, et al. (2009) found the following:

When students answer an in-class conceptual question individually using clickers, discuss it with their neighbors, and then revote on the same question, the percentage of correct answers typically increases. Our results indicate that peer discussion enhances understanding, even when none of the students in a discussion group originally knows the right answer.

The image on page 70 provides some strategies that can be used:

As a supplement to traditional discussion strategies, technology can serve as a catalyst to increase engagement by getting more learners actively involved during lessons. It can also take conversations to new levels of interactivity and expression. There are many great tools from which to choose, but we must be focused first on the improved outcomes that can result from purposeful use. Digital discussion:

- Allows creativity in responses (video, images, online research citations)

## Class Discussion Guidelines

| | | | | |
|---|---|---|---|---|
| **Accountable to the Learning Community** | **Listen** — Pay attention to the statements of others. | **Summarize** — Restate the ideas of a previous speaker in new language. | **Build** — Add to the statement of a previous speaker. | **Mark** — Direct attention to the importance of another's statement. |
| **Accountable to the Knowledge** | **Verify** — Check your understanding of previous statements & knowledge. | **Unpack** — Explain how you arrived at your answer. | **Support** — Give examples & evidence to support your answer. | **Link** — Point out the relationships among previous statements & knowledge. |
| **Accountable to Rigorous Thinking** | **Defend** — Defend your reasoning against a different point of view. | **Challenge** — Ask a previous speaker to explain & provide evidence for a statement. | **Combine** — Incorporate knowledge from multiple resources to form your ideas. | **Predict** — Draw conclusions about what might happen next, or as a result of ideas. |

Created by Angela Cunningham, Bullitt Central High School, Shepherdsville, KY 40165

- Provides an avenue for open reflection
- Affords more learners an opportunity to answer and ask questions
- Better meets the needs of shy and introverted students
- Can extend conversations and learning beyond the traditional school day
- Welcomes participation from others beyond the brick and mortar classroom
- Can be used to show parents and stakeholders the learning that is taking place
- Works to create a culture grounded in trust and responsibility

There is no replacement for great teaching. Sound pedagogy will always be at the heart of developing the ability of students to become disruptive thinkers. However, technology does enable some fascinating options that teachers can and should use to enhance learning for students. The main consideration when it comes to use is how it will fundamentally improve upon what has been done in the past. If this can be shown, then the possibilities are endless.

## Intentionally-Designed Thinking

No one can deny the fact that we are seeing some pretty exciting changes to teaching, learning, and leadership in many schools. Advances in research, brain science, and technology are opening up new and better pathways to reach learners like never before. This excitement in some cases is leading to change with supporting evidence of improvement. In other cases, money is being dumped into the latest tool, program, idea, or professional development without ensuring that instructional design is up to par in the first place. Let me repeat: Pedagogy trumps technology. It also goes without saying that a solid pedagogical foundation should be in place prior to implementing any "innovation."

Let's start by looking at practice from a general lens. To transform learning, we must also transform teaching. When looking at the image below where does current practice in your school or classroom fall? What immediate changes can be made to improve learning today for your students' tomorrow?

## Transforming Teaching

| Traditional Approach<br>**LOW AGENCY** | → | Transformed Approach<br>**HIGH AGENCY** |
|---|---|---|
| "Deliver" instruction | → | "Facilitate" learning |
| Teacher centered | → | Student centered |
| Classroom learning | → | Learning anytime/anywhere |
| Standardized approach | → | Personalized, differentiated |
| Learn to do | → | Do to learn |
| Content focused | → | Application focused |
| Looking for the right answer | → | Develop thinking |
| Teaching segmented curriculum | → | Integrating curriculum |
| Passive consumption | → | Active learning opportunities |

Eric Sheninger (@E_Sheninger)

Now let's turn our focus to specific elements of instruction. It is important to take a critical lens to our work to ensure efficacy if the goal is to improve learning. With that being said, it is incumbent upon all of us to make sure shifts to instructional design are occurring that result in better student outcomes. This is why a Return on Instruction (ROI) is so important, including both with and without the use of technology. It is important for educators to understand why this concept matters. When investing in technology, programs, professional development, and innovative ideas, there needs to be a Return on Instruction (ROI) that results in evidence of improved student learning outcomes (Sheninger & Murray, 2017).

The key to future-proofing education is getting kids to think in disruptive ways. "Easy" doesn't typically translate to learning. Challenging learners through complex problem solving and activities that involve critical thinking is extremely important, but they also must be afforded opportunities to apply their learning in authentic ways. This does not have to be an arduous process that takes up a great deal of time. Below are five areas to consider when implementing any digital tool or innovative idea to determine whether improvements to pedagogy are changing. Each area is followed by a question or two as a means to help self-assess where you are and if improvements can be made:

- *Level of questioning*: Are students being asked questions at the higher levels of the knowledge taxonomy? Do students have the opportunity to develop and then answer their own higher-order questions?
- *Authentic and/or interdisciplinary context*: Is there a connection to help students see why this learning is important and how it can be used outside of school?
- *Rigorous performance tasks*: Are students afforded an opportunity to actively apply what they have learned and create a product to demonstrate conceptual mastery aligned to standards?
- *Innovative assessment*: Are assessment practices changing to provide critical information about what students know or don't know? Are alternative forms of assessment being implemented, such as portfolios, to illustrate growth over time?
- *Improved Feedback*: Is feedback timely, aligned to standards, specific, and does it provide details on advancement towards a learning goal?

Improving learning outcomes relies on aligning instruction to solid research, ensuring that pedagogical shifts are occurring, holding ourselves (and others) accountable for growth, and showcasing evidence of improvement. By evaluating our practice we can determine where we are, but more importantly, where we actually want and need to be for our learners.

DISRUPTIVE
CHALLENGE #3

Videotape yourself (or a willing colleague) teaching a lesson to review what was taught and—more importantly—what was learned. Ask others to view and provide feedback. Using the *Transforming Teaching* image in this chapter as a guide, try to identify any areas of low-agency practice that you feel can be moved higher. Develop specific action steps that will allow for consistent integration into practice. Share theses reflections on social media using the #DisruptiveThink hashtag.

# CHAPTER 4

# Sticky Learning

*'I cannot teach anybody anything, I can only make them think."*
Socrates

A great deal has changed since I shifted my own thinking about learning in 2009. For starters, my primary device to connect on Twitter was a Blackberry. I didn't even have a Facebook page until a year later. Additionally, my views on education regarding teaching, learning, and leadership were beginning to evolve in ways that would eventually help our school experience success and recognition in many areas while also pushing my professional practice into a whole new dimension. As my thinking shifted, so did my views as to how education must change to better prepare learners to excel in a disruptive world.

## What Learners Really Need

When it comes to education, I now view it through two distinct lenses. On the one hand, there is my professional lens as I work with schools, districts, and organizations from all over the world. By looking at the rapid pace of change due in large part to advances in technology, past and present research on what actually works, and evidence of the impact that purposeful innovation can have on learning outcomes, we can gain valuable insights into what learners genuinely need. Then there is my parent lens. It is here where I try my best to look at the world through the eyes of my two children. It is impossible to predict what type of career path they will pursue at this point, which is why it is essential that their education helps them to develop critical competencies necessary for success in a future that is uncertain in so many ways.

The 21st Century skills discussion and debate has waged on even prior to the onset of this century. The ensuing conversations have provided an opportunity to critically evaluate what students need to know and be able to do in order to succeed in the new world of work. As we have moved further into this century the number "21" has less meaning, but the skills are still important. Thus, many educators now refer to these simply as "essential skills." Over time they have evolved beyond communication, collaboration, creativity, and critical thinking to include global awareness, entrepreneurship, and emerging technological proficiency.

One day I was speaking with Rose Else-Mitchell, my boss at the time, who pushed my thinking in this area. I raised the notion about what is needed now for success in the future, discussing skills students needed to be successful learners in the 21st Century and beyond. After looking at what I had listed and listening to my analysis, she commented that I was (or should be) referencing and explaining competencies, not just skills, students will need.

As I reflected on her feedback, I began to dive deeper into the difference between competencies and skills as well as their implications for learning. Let's look at an example. Most would agree that students should possess the following digital skills now and in the future:

+ Digital identity
+ Digital rights
+ Digital use
+ Digital safety

- Digital literacy
- Digital communication
- Digital social and emotional intelligence
- Digital security

As society becomes even more reliant on technology, we must equip our kids with all the above skills. Is that enough, though? Now let's take "digital" out of the picture and ask ourselves if being "skilled" in anything is good enough. As educators we need to shift our thinking in ways that align to a bigger picture. To accomplish this, we need to be more focused on how we can begin to address these as competencies to fully prepare students for success in a disruptive world.

While skills are an important part of learning and career paths, they're not rich or nuanced enough to guide students towards true mastery and enduring success. Skills focus on the "what" in terms of the abilities a student needs to perform a specific task or activity. They don't provide enough connection to the "how." Competencies take this to the next level by translating skills into *behaviors* that demonstrate what has been learned and mastered in a competent fashion. In short, skills identify the goal to be accomplished.

Competencies outline "how" the goals and objectives will be accomplished. They are more detailed and define the requirements for success in broader, more inclusive terms than skills do. There is also an increased level of depth within competencies that encompasses skills, knowledge, and abilities. To succeed in the new world of work, students will need to demonstrate the right mix of skills, knowledge, and on-the-job agility. A skill is a practical or cognitive demonstration of what a student can do. Competency is the proven use of skills, knowledge, and abilities to demonstrate mastery of learning by solving problems.

Let's look at an example for more clarity. A person can become an effective presenter through practice, learning from others, and studying resources, but in order to be a strong communicator one must rely on a combination of skills PLUS behavior and knowledge. A strong communicator possesses advanced language skills, the knowledge of diverse cultures, and behaves patiently when communicating. In short, skills are specific learned activities like mopping the floor, using a computer, and stocking merchandise, while competencies are skills + knowledge + behaviors including problem solving, communication, and professionalism.

Success in the future will rely on much more than possessing skills in isolation. It's time to shift our focus and energy to developing and assessing core and innovative competencies that will serve students throughout their lives.

We must focus on sound pedagogy while creating a culture that truly prepares learners with the qualities they need now and well into the future. It is here where learners have the competence to think in complex ways while being able to readily apply learning authentically. Even when confronted with perplexing unknowns, they can leverage their knowledge and expertise to create solutions and take action needed for success in a rapidly changing world. What students need are competencies in the areas of creativity, reflection, teamwork, active participation, time management, and inquiry:

**Creative thinkers** generate and explore ideas and make original connections. They try different ways to tackle a problem, working with others to find imaginative solutions and outcomes that are of value.

**Reflective learners** evaluate their strengths and limitations, setting realistic goals with criteria for success. They monitor their performance and progress, inviting feedback from others and making changes to further their learning.

**Collaborative workers** engage confidently with others, adapting to different contexts and taking responsibility for their own role on the team. They listen to and take into account different perspectives. They form collaborative relationships, resolving issues to reach agreed-upon outcomes.

**Active participators** readily explore issues that affect them and those around them. They actively engage in the life of their school, college, workplace, or wider community by taking responsible action to improve others as well as themselves.

**Self-managers** organize themselves, showing personal responsibility, initiative, creativity, and enterprise with a commitment to learning and self-improvement. They actively embrace change, respond positively to new priorities, cope with challenges and look for opportunities to grow.

**Autonomous inquirers** process and evaluate information in their investigations, planning what to do and how to go about it. They make informed and well-reasoned decisions, while recognizing that others may have different beliefs and attitudes.

As someone who has transitioned from the public to the private sector, I can tell you without hesitation that the qualities and outcomes listed above are critical in my current role. A strong case can also be made that our learners would benefit greatly if these were emphasized across the curriculum. Our learners are relying on us to provide them with an education that will withstand the test of time.

Think about where you are in relation to these competencies, but more importantly, where you want to be. How does learning in your classroom, school, or district help learners become creative thinkers, reflective learners, collaborative workers, active participators, self-managers, and autonomous inquirers? Where is there an opportunity for growth?

It is also important to remember how these qualities and outcomes are just as vital to you as they are for the students you serve. As you reflect, think about where you can grow in these areas to benefit both professionally and personally.

## Gauging Thinking

There are wide-ranging thoughts about what constitutes authentic learning. From these conversations, educators form their own perspectives and opinions that best align with the vision, mission, and goals of their classroom, school, or district. However, consensus is critical if the goal is scalable change that results in improved learning outcomes for students. Research and evidence should play a significant role in what learning can and should be as well as whether it is actually taking place. A common vision, shared language, and clear expectations go a long way toward creating a vibrant learning culture. When it comes to learning, consider two critically-important questions:

1. Are kids thinking at increasingly high levels of the knowledge taxonomy?
2. How are kids applying their thinking in relevant ways?

A focus on disruptive thinking provides a practical way to determine the answers to both of these questions by looking at the level of questioning and the tasks in which kids are engaged. Consider it a litmus test of sorts. Where does the instruction (what the teacher does) and the learning (what the student does) fall in terms of lesson activities? Good instruction can, and should, lead to empowered learning, with movement along both the thinking and application continuums. When technology is added to the mix, it should be used purposefully by the learner in ways that address the two questions posed above.

I cannot reiterate how important it is to get kids to think in disruptive ways. The world today is influenced by advanced robotics and autonomous transport, artificial intelligence and machine learning, advanced materials, biotechnology, and genomics. These developments

> Don't prepare learners for something. Prepare them for anything.

continue to transform the way we live and the way we work. Some jobs disappear, while new ones are created. Then there are those that don't even exist today but will eventually become commonplace. What is certain is that the future workforce will need to align its mindset and skillset to keep pace with evolving demands. The lesson learned is as simple as it is profound: Don't prepare learners for something. Prepare them for anything.

To accomplish this, we must focus on cognitive flexibility, the ability to shift our thoughts and adapt our behavior to the changing environment. In other words, one's ability to disengage from a previous task and respond effectively to a new one. It's a faculty that most of us take for granted, yet an essential competency for navigating life. Another way of looking at it is "developing means to spontaneously restructure one's knowledge, in many ways, in adaptive response to radically changing situational demands" (Spiro & Jehn 1990, P. 65).

In my mind, cognitive flexibility might be the most important competency that educators can help learner's develop because it incorporates so many of the others in some form or another. Below are a few ideas and strategies for helping learners develop this important element:

1. Design learning activities to support divergent thinking where learners demonstrate understanding in creative and non-conventional ways.
2. Empower students to identify a problem and then come up with a workable solution.
3. Allow students to explore a topic of interest then demonstrate what they have learned through non-traditional assessments.
4. Implement personalized learning opportunities where students think critically, openly explore, and pursue areas of passion, using their own intuitive ideas to learn in powerful ways.
5. Engage students in a real-world application in unanticipated situations where they use their knowledge to tackle problems that have more than one solution.

6.  Provide pathways for students to transfer learning to a new context.

How we prepare our learners for the new world of work must become a problem of practice for all schools. The key to future-proofing education and learning is getting kids to think by engaging them in tasks that develop cognitive flexibility.

## Ownership Through Inquiry

As a child, I was enamored by nature. My twin brother and I were always observing and collecting any and all types of critters we could get our hands on. Growing up in a rural area of northwestern New Jersey made it quite easy to seek out and find different plants and animals on a daily basis. We would spend countless hours roaming around the woods, corn fields, ponds, and streams in our quest to study as much local wildlife as possible. It's no wonder that I eventually became a science teacher since my surroundings growing up played a major role in my eventual decision to go into the field of education.

To this day, I still can't believe my mother tolerated us bringing an array of animals into the house. For years, my brother and I were particularly interested in caterpillars. We would use encyclopedias and field guides to identify certain species that were native to our area. Through our research, we determined what each caterpillar ate and subsequently scoured trees, bushes, and other plants in our quest to collect, observe, and compare the differences between species. We even kept journals with notes and sketches. When we were successful in locating these insects, we then collected them in jars. Our research ensured that each species had the correct type of food as well as appropriate physical requirements to either make a chrysalis (butterflies) or cocoon (moths).

In the case of moths, some were in their cocoons for months. Hence, my brother and I stored these jars under our beds. At times we forgot that we had these living creatures under them until at night when we heard them flapping their wings and moving around the jars after emerging from their cocoons. I can only imagine what my parents thought of this, but am thankful they supported our inquiry in so many ways, from having encyclopedias available for research to providing us with the autonomy to harness our intrinsic motivation to learn. Through it all, our observations led to questions and together my brother and I worked to find answers. Even though we were not always successful in this endeavor, the journey was worth it. Questions upon questions drove the inquiry process for both of us and from there we leveraged available resources and synthesized what we had learned.

The story above is an example of how my brother and I embarked upon an informal learning process driven by inquiry. We owned the process from start to finish and our parents acted as indirect facilitators through their support and encouragement. Both inquiry and owner-ship of learning are not new concepts, although they are often thrown around interchangeably lately, especially "ownership." Deborah Voltz and Margaret Damiano-Lantz came up with this description:

> Ownership of learning refers to the development of a sense of con-nectedness, active involvement, and personal investment in the learning process. This is important for all learners in that it facili-tates understanding and retention and promotes a desire to learn. (1993, p. 19)

After reading this description, I can't help but see the alignment to the story shared above. We learned not because we *had* to, but because we *wanted* to. Herein lies a potential issue in schools: Are kids learning because they are intrinsically motivated to learn or are they compelled to through a system which encourages compliance and conformity? The former results when learners have a real sense of ownership. There are many ways to empower kids to own their learning. Often, we are told that technology can be such a catalyst. In many cases this is true, but ownership can result if the conditions are established in which stu-dents inquire by way of their own observations and questions. WNET Education describes inquiry as follows:

*"Inquiry" is defined as "a seeking for truth, information, or knowl-edge — seeking information by questioning." Individuals carry on the process of inquiry from the time they are born until they die. Through the process of inquiry, individuals construct much of their understanding of the natural and human-designed worlds. Inquiry implies a "need or wants to know" premise. Inquiry is not so much seeking the right answer—because often there is none — but rather seeking appropriate resolutions to questions and issues.* (2004, para. 2)

The first sentence ties in directly to the concept of ownership, but we also see the importance of questioning. This is why empow-ering learners to develop their own questions and then use an array of resources to process and share new knowledge or demonstrating an understanding of concepts are critical if ownership of learning is the goal. Inquiry supports and drives thinking where memorization does not. Memorization can eventually even get in the way of learning, yet the practice continues in schools.

Fortunately, the sciences provide schools and educators with many natural opportunities to move away from the boring, monotonous task of memorizing facts and information to a more constructivist approach associated with inquiry-based learning. I was always in awe of Tahreen Chowdhury, a teacher at New Milford High School in New Jersey where I served as principal. She embraced inquiry in her classroom as a way to motivate her students to learn as much as possible. One day her chemistry classes conducted testing on various consumer products. While the students were learning about acids and bases, they con-ducted a simulation where their task was to create solutions of differ-ent pH. They also worked with another simulation that demonstrated acids and bases at a molecular level.

Based on their learning from the two simulations, and with the facilitation of Ms. Chowdhury, students discussed a design for testing different brands of antacids. They knew they needed a sample acid and a pH indicator. The students were given lemon juice as acid, grape juice as base, and they tested three different brands of antacid (*Equate* regular strength, *Equate* maximum strength, and *Rolaids*). The students hypothesized that the grape juice (pH indicator) would change color when enough of the antacid had been added to neutralize the acid. They recorded the number of drops used from each brand of antacid, and determined that *Rolaids* was the best among the three based on their results.

Ms. Chowdhury believed that experiments such as this help students contextualize their learning at a more practical level than merely memorizing the definitions of acids and bases. The students also thoroughly enjoyed any hands-on activities. Regardless of the level of the course, students today need to be provided opportunities to think disruptively. Memorization of facts does not allow for students to truly grasp concepts, let alone apply them and demonstrate mastery. Science is inherently primed for inquiry-based learning, but educators can promote this pedagogical technique across all content areas.

It's all about raising the bar when it comes to getting kids to think. When activities are developed appropriately, students are afforded the opportunity to construct new knowledge through exploration, problem solving, developing then answering their own questions, application, and trial and error. Such techniques typically make students uncomfortable at first, because they have become conditioned by our traditional culture of education to prefer being spoon fed information instead of having to think for themselves. Not only do students fight such techniques at first, but, often, so do their parents. This stems from the fact that many parents want their children taught the same way they were taught. I have engaged in numerous conversations over the years with parents, explaining to them how the inquiry-based process for learning will much better prepare their children for future success. It is a conversation that I relish, as the students themselves ultimately discover the value of this type of learning over traditional pedagogical techniques that are mostly passive in nature and do not require critical thought.

Ms. Chowdury evolved into a master teacher in physics using this approach and here is why. Physics is often thought to be a fun subject where students get to perform exciting experiments. Ms. Chowdhury had a teaching philosophy that her students could not engage in fun activities simply for the sake of having fun, but they should engage in fun activities during which learning was the primary purpose. When her students discovered that she had some Nerf guns in the classroom, they wanted to play with them. So, she created an assignment involving Nerf guns requiring students to apply their understanding of energy concepts to figure out the velocity of the bullet as it was leaving the gun.

She gave her students a meter stick, a protractor with a string attached from the center, and a Nerf gun with one "bullet." The students' task was to design how they wanted to set up and use the materials to be able to calculate the starting velocity of the bullet. The students chose to use the protractor to figure out how high the bullet went and from there apply the concepts of energy to calculate velocity. When it comes to learning, there should never be an easy way out. Making the process fun and engaging while invoking problem solving and critical thinking skills epitomizes the type of learning our students need and deserve.

Ownership through inquiry is not as difficult as you might think if there is a common vision, language, expectation, and a commitment to student agency. Begin by simply bumping up the level of questions as part of the inquiry process while empowering kids to demonstrate understanding aligned with relevant contexts.

## The Power of Scaffolding

Over the years, I have worked with many schools and districts in the role of a coach. Most of this work is focused on digital pedagogy, so naturally, I am observing and collecting evidence to get a handle on both the level of instruction and the learning that is taking place. To allow educators to critically reflect on their practice, I take many pictures of what I see, especially the types of learning activities in which students are engaged. After numerous visits, we all debrief and discuss the effective practices observed, while also highlighting areas needing improvement.

The message I try to convey is that technology should not be separate from sound instructional design, but, instead, serve as a ubiquitous entity that supports or enhances curriculum, instruction, and assessment as appropriate. The five main components of sound instructional design that I tend to focus on during debriefing conversations include: level of questioning, authentic or interdisciplinary contexts, rigorous performance tasks, innovative assessments, and improved feedback. Of these five components, questioning techniques are something teachers and administrators can work to improve in every lesson.

Here is what I struggle with based on what I actually see in practice. In many cases, the "wow" factor of technology is placed ahead of getting kids to think deeply or authentically apply their learning. Take tools like *Kahoot* and *Quizizz*. There are no inherent issues with the tools themselves; educators just have to be more mindful of how they are being used. Many of these tools add either a fun or competitive factor to the process of answering low-level, multiple-choice questions. Foundational knowledge is still important. However, if this is the only way tools like these are used, then we are missing a golden opportunity to challenge our learners to think deeply about concepts.

While conducting some coaching visits at an elementary school, I saw a teacher using *Quizizz*. At first glance, all I saw were student responses to knowledge-based questions on the interactive whiteboard (IWB) to check for understanding. What I saw next really made me smile. With the students sitting on the floor around the IWB, the teacher displayed the *Quizziz* results and then had the kids explain why they answered the way they did. This is a simple, yet powerful, example of scaffolding and building on the content. As mentioned previously, foundational knowledge provides a bridge to higher-level thinking and application. When using response-based technologies, the key is to make sure that the level of questioning is addressed through scaffolding techniques. The same can be said in regard to any type of activity without technology.

Scaffolding refers to a variety of instructional techniques used to move students progressively toward stronger understanding and, ultimately, greater independence in the learning process. Questioning is an integral component of this process. Historically, teachers have asked questions to check what has been learned and understood, to help them gauge whether to further review previous learning, to increase or decrease the challenge, and to assess whether students are ready to move forward and learn new information. This can be structured as a simple "teacher versus the class" approach where the teacher asks a question and accepts an answer from a volunteer or selects a specific student to answer. These approaches are implicit in any pedagogy, but teachers need a range of "open" questioning strategies to address different learning needs and situations. Teachers must also pitch questions effectively to raise the thinking challenge and to target specific students or groups within the class.

The image on page 89 illustrates how to scaffold for disruptive thinking:

By examining instructional design, improvement can happen now. Curiosity and passion reside in all learners. Inquiry can be used to tap into both of these elements and, in the process, students will be empowered to own their learning.

## The Learning Pit

It all comes back to a simple, yet profound question: what is the purpose of education? To many, this might seem like a ridiculous question with the answer being quite obvious. But is it? Some might suggest that the ability to recall or memorize facts and information is a fundamental purpose of education. The casual observer might then anoint anyone who is able to do this effectively as smart or intelligent. Perhaps he or she is. But is being able to ace a standardized test an accurate indicator of what someone knows, can do, or both?

For each individual student, there exists a unique path for acquiring, applying, and constructing new knowledge. It is much more challenging to accomplish this than some might think, and the journey is often convoluted. Yet, the fact remains that learning is anything but linear. It is more about the process than arriving at a particular destination.

**DISRUPTIVE THINKING** (vertical arrow)

**LEVEL 4**
How would you design a...to ...?
How would you compose a song about...?
How would you rewrite the ending to the story?
What would be different today, if that event occurred as...?
Can you see a possible solution to...?
How could you teach that to others?
If you had access to all the resources, how would you deal with...?
What new and unusual invention would you create for...?
What authentic solution can you develop to solve this problem?
Can you predict what will happen next and why?

**LEVEL 3**
How are these similar/different?
How is this like...?
What's another way we could say/explain/express that?
What do you think are some reasons/causes that...?
Why did.....changes occur?
What is a better solution to...?
How would you defend your position about that?

**LEVEL 2**
Would you do that?
Where will you use that knowledge?
How does that relate to your experience?
What observations relate to...?
Where would you locate that information?
How would you illustrate that?
How would you interpret that?
How would you collect that data?
How do you know it works?

**LEVEL 1**
What is/are...?
How many...?
How do/does...?
What did you observe...?
What else can you tell me about...?
What does it mean...?
What can you recall...?
Where did you find that...?
Who is/are...?
How would you define that in your own terms?

When you think about the greatest minds in our society, perception is rarely reality. If you take a close look and peel away the layers, you will see a path fraught with challenges, frustration, and failure. The same can be said about any person who actively solves problems on a daily basis such as carpenters, electricians, plumbers, and auto mechanics. What do they all have in common? Each and every one has been able to utilize disruptive thinking to apply what he or she knows in order to solve an array of problems.

Regardless of where a student is at in their learning pathway, it is incumbent to challenge him or her through authentic experiences. A focus on disruptive thinking can provide teachers and administrators with the context to create and evaluate both questions and tasks that empower cognitive flexibility and application while fostering relationships in the process. So, what does this look like? One of my favorite images that illustrate what the process should look like is the learning pit seen below:

The questions throughout the journey are key, in my opinion. If learning is not rigorous and relevant, then students can most likely jump right over the pit. That's what I mean when I say if it is easy, then it probably isn't learning. What this ultimately equates to are questions and tasks that don't challenge kids to think and apply what they are learning across multiple disciplines or to solve either real-world predictable to unpredictable problems. When all these elements are part of a lesson or project, we enhance the development of cognitive flexibility within our students.

Nothing comes easy in life. There is no better way to teach this life-long lesson than getting kids into the learning pit to experience the disruptive dip before ultimately coming out more confident and capable.

## Performance Tasks

Pedagogy is always at the forefront of my thinking about the work we do. Decades of research have laid the foundation for current studies that bring to light how we can improve teaching, learning, and leadership.

We must not lose sight of pedagogical practices that work. With all the great ideas educators are exposed to thanks to social media, as well as virtual and live events, it is essential that we pause to reflect on what it takes to move from what sounds good in theory to examples of successful implementation. Ideas shouldn't just "seem" right. They must be based on evidence rooted in students achieving and performing at high levels as a result of the practice.

When I served as a principal, we wanted to transform the learning culture of the school. For years, our students, like many others across the world, just "did" school. Learning was more or less a monotonous task consisting of the same types of activities and assessments that occurred over and over again. We weren't consistently pushing our students to think deeply or authentically apply what they had learned. Getting in classrooms more and taking a critical lens to our work helped us take the needed steps to raise the learning bar and expect more from our students. We began by improving the level of questioning across the board. From there, our focus was on the development of performance tasks that took into account objectives, learning targets, and curriculum alignment. This approach pushed more of our students where we wanted them: into the learning pit.

Performance tasks afford students an opportunity to actively apply what they have learned and create a product to demonstrate conceptual understanding aligned to standards. Jay McTighe describes performance tasks as follows:

> *A performance task is any learning activity or assessment that asks students to perform to demonstrate their knowledge, understanding, and proficiency. Performance tasks yield a tangible product or performance that serve as evidence of learning. Unlike a selected-response item (e.g., multiple-choice or matching) that asks students to select from given alternatives, a performance task presents a situation that calls for learners to apply their learning in context.* (2015, para. 1).

Learning in highly successful schools enables students to know what to do even when they don't know what to do. This is also referred to as cognitive flexibility discussed earlier, the mental ability to switch between thinking about two different concepts and to think about multiple ideas simultaneously. To gain that competence, students need to acquire a depth of knowledge and a rich set of skills and then be taught how to apply their skills/knowledge to unpredictable situations in the world beyond school. This is critical if we are to fully prepare students for the new world of work.

With a focus on disruptive thinking, educators can begin to develop performance tasks that push learners to demonstrate understanding while applying what has been learned in relevant contexts. McTighe identifies seven characteristics to consider:

1. Performance tasks call for the application of knowledge and skills, not just recall or recognition.
2. Performance tasks are open-ended and typically do not yield a single, correct answer.
3. Performance tasks establish novel and authentic contexts for performance.
4. Performance tasks provide evidence of understanding via transfer.
5. Performance tasks are multi-faceted.
6. Performance tasks can integrate two or more subjects as well as 21st-century skills.
7. Performances on open-ended tasks are evaluated with established criteria and rubrics. (2015, para. 4).

The GRASPS model (Wiggins & McTighe, 2004) can greatly assist educators in the construction of quality performance tasks in alignment. The **GRASPS** acronym stands for the following: **G**oals, **R**ole, **A**udience, **S**ituation, **P**roducts or **P**erformances, and **S**tandards.

It is important to remember that the two critical elements in any quality performance task are evidence of learning and relevant application. Performance tasks push students to think more deeply about their learning while developing a greater sense of relevance beyond the classroom.

One of my fondest memories of school was my science teacher, Mr. South. Having attended a K-8 consolidated school in rural NJ, we knew who all the teachers were. However, Mr. South stood out. I still remember as an elementary student seeing paper flyers with a caricature of Mr. South wearing one of his famous flannel shirts.

There was a reason why everyone talked about Mr. South. He was an amazing teacher. Every student in the school looked forward to taking his class. Since our school was small, there was even a chance

| Goals | Role | Audience | Situation | Products | Standards |
|-------|------|----------|-----------|----------|-----------|
| Your task is... | You are... | Your client is... | The context you find yourself in is... | You will create... in order to... | Your performance or product needs to... |
| The goal is to... | You have been asked to... | Your target audience is... | The challenge involves dealing with... | You will need to develop... so that... | Your work will be judged by... |
| The problem or challenge is to... | Your job is... | You need to convince... | | | Your product must meet the following standards... |
| The obstacle to overcome is... | | | | | A successful result will... |

From *Understanding by Design, Expanded 2nd Edition*, By Grant Wiggins and Jay McTighe, Alexandria, VA: ASCD. © 2005 by ASCD. Reprinted with permission. All rights reserved.

you could have him multiple times before moving up to the high school. What separated Mr. South from his colleagues was his passion for helping students learn and his love of the sciences. His lessons were light

> He didn't *teach* science. We *learned* science.

on direct instruction and heavy on authentic connections and application. He didn't *teach* science. We *learned* science.

Mr. South is the main reason I pursued a degree in science initially, before taking this passion to the field of education. There was one project in particular that has stuck with me to this day. Instead of lecturing to us about Mars, he had us actually create Mars in the classroom. Students were divided into groups with different tasks to complete. Each specific task of each group played a part in the overall Martian project. My partner and I were tasked with getting materials to Mars in order to create an infrastructure on the planet. Through our research we came across a device called the mass driver. We presented our findings to Mr. South and he gave us the task of creating two different working mass driver prototypes.

During and after school, my partner and I worked on developing these miniature prototypes that would actually propel mass. This was certainly a frustrating experience, as we were never really asked to learn like this before. Countless hours were spent outside of school working on this project. We even went to Mr. South's house on weekends so that we could use the many different tools he had in his garage. Through it all, we owned our learning by being engaged in thoughtful work and made numerous connections to other disciplines. The process in itself was fraught with highs and lows, but in the end, we developed the two working prototypes as assigned while learning with our hands.

Over a period of weeks, each group worked to complete their assigned tasks as well as a research paper. The final step was then to actually create Mars in the classroom and that is what Mr. South had us do. It was controlled learning chaos that involved tools, wood, Papier-mâché, collaboration, communication, black lights, and so much more. Once the surface of Mars was completed, each group set up stations throughout the planet to present their specific projects. The culminating activity was a multi-night presentation to parents and the greater community during which each group showed off a thriving society that would hypothetically be created on Mars.

This was by far one of the most powerful learning experiences I ever engaged in as a student. Mr. South had us actively learn science instead of just taking notes followed by a traditional assessment. It was relevant, meaningful, and fun. We developed the competence to think in complex ways and to authentically apply knowledge and skills. Even when faced with perplexing unknowns, the pedagogy employed by Mr. South allowed us to use extensive knowledge and skills we didn't even know we had to create solutions and take action, acquiring critical competencies along the way.

Many of the competencies needed today were evident in this project that took place in 1988. It is not that this type of learning is new. In fact, nothing we see and hear for the most part is new. What has changed is how technology provides a new avenue to actively integrate this type of learning in ways that many of us could never have imagined. The key is to focus on project-based and authentic inquiry.

## The Point of a Lesson

I have never been a huge fan of collecting and reviewing teachers' lesson plans. It is my opinion that you can learn a great deal more by collecting and looking at assessments. Regardless of where you stand on the lesson plan debate, intent is what really matters. For all of us who have taught or have served in a leadership position that supports teachers, I suspect we would agree that the point of any lesson is to help students learn. Yes, there are standards and curriculum to cover as well as essential concepts. There are activities, projects, and assessments along the way. In some cases, innovative techniques such as a more personal or blended approach might be the preferred pedagogical pathway. No matter what constitutes a lesson plan, the goal remains the same: learning.

If the intended outcome is clear to us, the same must be said for our learners. This begs a fundamental question we should always consider: do students understand the point of the lesson? If not, then it is challenging to meet any goals that are set. It all begins with a clear articulation of learning outcomes. For many of us, this comes in the form of objectives. I know when I went through my coursework and teaching certification process, writing clear objectives was emphasized as a critical component of any lesson plan. As I entered the classroom, what I was taught carried over and objectives were not only included in every lesson plan I developed, but I also listed them on the board for students to see. Although it is not always necessary that objectives be posted for all to see, it is crucial that students understand the intended learning outcomes of every lesson.

In my coaching work, I now advise educators to move away from this traditional component of lesson design and implementation. Objectives, if we really think about them, are more often what the adult wants to achieve in terms of alignment to standards and concepts as well as scope and sequence. Just look at how they are written and see if you feel the same way. Learning targets, on the other hand, frame the lesson from the students' point of view and are written using "I can" or "I will" statements. They help learners grasp the lesson's purpose, including why it is crucial to learn a particular chunk of information or concept, on this day, and in this way. Quality learning targets as part of an effective lesson help students answer these three questions:

1. Why did we learn this and what will I be able to do when I've finished this lesson?
2. What idea, topic, or subject is important for me to learn and understand so that I can do this?
3. How will I show that I can do this, and how well will I have to do it to demonstrate that I have learned something new?

Developing learning targets does not go far enough though. Learners need to understand the point of a lesson just as much as a teacher or administrator. Imparting relevance through a specific context and application helps achieve this. However, everything must be tied together from the learner's point of view. This is why closure and reflection at the end of the lesson are crucial. Either or both of these elements can be tied to the use of a KWL chart. Here is an updated and expanded version of such a chart:

| K | W | H | L | A | Q |
|---|---|---|---|---|---|
| What do I **know**?<br><br>Why is it important that I **know** this? | What do I **want** to know?<br><br>Why do I **want** to know this? | **How** do I find out? | What have I **learned**?<br><br>How will I use what I have **learned**? | What **action** will I take and why? | What **questions** do I have?<br><br>How will I **answer** these or what **assistance** do I need to answer them? |

From a pedagogical standpoint, it is vital to build these into daily learning activities to bring the learning process full circle. Bottom line: everyone—especially our students—should understand the point of a lesson.

## Movement Enhances Thinking

Spending time in schools as a leadership and learning coach has been some of the most gratifying work I have done. The best part is the conversations that I get to have with learners, especially at the elementary level. These always leave me invigorated and remind me why I became a teacher many years ago. Then there is the practicality of being able to work with both administrators and teachers at the ground level to improve pedagogy and, in turn, student outcomes. From this lens, I am able to see the seeds of change germinate into real shifts in practice. It also provides me with an opportunity to reflect on what I see and my take on how the field of education can continue to evolve in ways that better support the needs of all learners.

Case in point: One day I was participating in learning walks at an elementary school. As we entered, the lesson was about to conclude. The teacher had students engaged in a closure activity to demonstrate an understanding of math multiplication concepts. After the exit tickets were collected, the teacher had all students participate in a brain break activity. Each child was instructed to get up, walk around the room, and find a partner who was not in their pre-assigned seating group. They were then instructed to compete in several games of rock-paper-scissors with various peers. After some heightened physical activity and fun, the lesson then transitioned to a do-now activity where students completed a science table to review prior learning.

I have long been enamored by the concept of brain breaks. As a result, I did a little digging into the concept. Numerous studies have found that without periodic breaks, students have higher instances of inappropriate classroom behavior. Elisabeth Trambley (2017) conducted her own research study to determine the impact of brain breaks on behavior. She found that once the breaks were implemented, inappropriate behavior diminished, establishing a functional relationship between breaks and classroom behavior.

The concept of brain breaks prompted me to think about a growing trend in education. As students progress through the K-12 system, there is less and less movement built into their day. I have seen this firsthand in schools across the globe. Research reviewed by Elisabeth Trambley, Jacob Sattelmair & John Ratey (2009), and Kristy Ford (2016) concludes that both recess and physical activity lead to improved learning outcomes. Studies have also found that movement improves overall learning as well as test scores, skills, and content knowledge in core subjects such as mathematics and reading fluency as well as increases in student interest and motivation (Adams-Blair & Oliver, 2011; Braniff, 2011; Vazou et al., 2012; Erwin, Fedewa, & Ahn, 2013; Browning et al., 2014).

Not only is physical education an absolute must in the K-12 curriculum, but schools need to do more to ensure that movement is being integrated into all classes. Need more proof on how important movement is? All one has to do is to turn to science. The brain needs regular stimulation to properly function and this can come in the form of exercise or movement. Based on what is now known about the brain, it is an effective cognitive strategy to improve memory and retrieval, strengthen learning, and enhance motivation among all learners.

Below is a brief list of simple ideas for incorporating movement into the school day:

+ Add more recess time, not just in elementary, but in middle schools as well.
+ Intentionally incorporate movement activities into each lesson, regardless of the age of your students. Build in the time but don't let the activity dictate what you are going to do. Monitor your learners' needs and be flexible in determining the most appropriate activity.
+ Implement short brain breaks from thirty seconds to two minutes in length every twenty minutes or so that incorporate physical activity into the lesson. If technology is available use tools such as GoNoodle (www.gonoodle.com), which is a popular way for students to rotate between stations in a blended learning environment. If not, no sweat. A practical activity can simply be getting students to walk in place or stand up and perform stretching routines.
+ Ensure every student is enrolled in physical education during the school day.

Don't look at kids moving in class as a poor use of instructional time. As shown from the research above, movement is an essential component of learning. If the goal is to help kids become better disruptive thinkers, then we must be intentional about getting them up and moving in school.

## Reflective Learning

The quest to improve pedagogy and, in turn, learner outcomes, is a focus of many schools. We toil away at chasing the next big innovative idea, trend, or tool as a path to improvement, yet little changes. Maybe success lies in taking a more discerning look at our daily practices. The key to future-proofing education is to empower students to not only think, but also to apply their thinking in authentic ways to demonstrate what has been learned. Whether you call this rigorous learning, deeper learning, personalized learning, or just plain learning is of no concern to me. Semantics aside, the goal of all schools should be to equip students with the appropriate knowledge, skills, mindset, and behaviors to help them develop into competent learners. Getting better at this should be our rallying cry.

We can have students "learn to do" or we can flip the experience, having them "do to learn." The question then becomes not a conversation as to which pathway is better, but whether learning has occurred. Sure, we can slap a grade on it and in many cases that becomes evidence that learning did or did not happen, but there are flaws inherent here. Unfortunately, many grading practices are entirely arbitrary and do not provide an accurate indication of learning; we need to rethink our traditional grading practices. We may not be able to completely do away with grades or tests; that may not be realistic right now (although, it might be at some point in the future, one hopes). The more important question for now is simply, what can be integrated into daily practice to help students learn?

To get to where you want to be, you need to be honest about where you are right now. Are your students provided an opportunity during every lesson to reflect on what they have learned? As John Dewey stated, "We do not learn from experience; we learn from reflecting on experience." It is not unreasonable to ask that we provide students opportunities to reflect on the learning target for the day. As I work with schools and districts, my main area of focus is to help improve pedagogy, both with and without the use of technology. Unfortunately, I rarely see opportunities for student reflection during countless walk-throughs, lesson plan reviews, or audits measuring how digital tools are being used in classrooms. This is an easy fix if an approach is taken where there is a combination of self-efficacy and commitment to a school-wide goal. Costa & Kallick share why reflection is a critical component of the learning process:

> Reflection has many facets. For example, reflecting on work enhances its meaning. Reflecting on experiences encourages insight and complex learning. We foster our growth when we control our learning, so some reflection is best done alone. Reflection is also enhanced, however, when we ponder our learning with others. Reflection involves linking a current experience to previous learnings (a process called scaffolding). Reflection also involves drawing forth cognitive and emotional information from several sources: visual, auditory, kinesthetic, and tactile. To reflect, we must act upon and process the information, synthesizing and evaluating the data. In the end, reflecting also means applying what we've learned to contexts beyond the original situations in which we learned something. (2008, para. 2)

Something as simple as intentionally planning for student reflection opportunities within the school day has the potential to significantly improve learning. Reflective learning is a way of allowing students to step back from their learning experience to help them develop disruptive thinking skills and improve future performance by analyzing their learning experiences. This type of learning helps move the student from surface level to deep learning. Daily reflection provides students with an opportunity to exert more ownership over their learning.

Below are some simple strategies that can be used to integrate reflection into any lesson:

- **Writing** - A daily journal or blog can be added as a means to not just review, but also reflect, on prior learning. It can also be used as a form of closure. Simple reflective prompts can also be used. A great deal of research reviewed by Lew & Schmidt (2011) suggests the positive impact of reflective writing on cognitive development.

- **Video** – *Flipgrid* fever has overtaken many schools. This tool can allow students to use video to reflect on their learning. They can be guided with simple prompts. The videos are then easily accessible for review on a grid. Think about the value of having students see and hear from their peers about what they learned or struggled with during the lesson. In their research, Rose et al. (2016) found that video made the reflection experience more authentic and meaningful for both student and teacher. There are many ways educators can harness the power of video to enhance learning.

- **Peer interaction** – Research by Hatton & Smith (1995) indicated that engaging with another person in a way that encourages talking with, questioning, or confronting, helps the reflective process by placing the learner in a safe environment so that self-revelation may take place. Consider implementing the critical friends' strategy where students provide peer critiques of each other's thinking or more opportunities for discussion as a means to reflect. Using peer critiques to evaluate and improve student work is a natural outgrowth of the movement toward more authentic assessments in education (Henderson & Karr-Kidwell, 1998).

Making time for students to reflect on their learning leads to more ownership of the process, builds essential connections between both present and past experiences, provides teachers with valuable information related to standards attainment or mastery, and compels them to exert a degree of self-management as they become more capable of regulating their own learning. With these positive outcomes, reflective learning should become the new normal in our schools.

## Thinking Through Play

As a kid I loved to play. I spent countless hours building forts in the woods, creating sandcastles at the beach, riding bikes, playing Atari (then Nintendo, Game Boy, Sega Genesis, etc.) or just running around for no apparent reason. Kids love play and it is a central component of their social and emotional development. Important qualities such as patience, compromise, focus,, problem solving, determination, and resourcefulness, to name a few, are developed through play. Not only are these qualities vital to success, but they also represent elements that cannot be tested. Here is a short list:

- Curiosity
- Sense of wonder
- Creativity
- Persistence
- Growth mindset
- Enthusiasm
- Leadership
- Courage
- Civic-mindfulness
- Self-discipline
- Empathy
- Grace
- Motivation
- Reliability
- Compassion
- Humor
- Resilience
- Disruptive thinking

As much as I loved to play as a child, I think I enjoy watching how it impacts others, including my own children, even more. My kids engage in play in unique ways based on their personalities. As a child, my son Nick was an avid gamer who loved *Minecraft* and the creative freedom it fostered. On most nights we would see him with his headset on, collaborating and communicating with kids his age from across the country, and utilizing thought and strategy to create a product that mattered to him. He also had a passion for basketball, golf, Nerf gun battles, laser tag, going to the park, and, of course, playing with his sister. They enjoyed walking the neighborhood together, engaged in *Pokemon Go*. I loved it when they came back and told me how many kilometers they walked while having fun.

My daughter, Isabella, on the other hand, was a ball of raw energy. She was always on the go, running around the house and outside when the Texas heat was in check. Like her brother, technology was a huge component of her play regime. Many evenings after dinner she retreated to her room to play *Roblox* with her best friend, Brooke, who lived in New York. She would have a computer set up for the game and then stream in Brooke live using Facetime on her iPad Mini. They then played the game together, laughing and conversing in real-time. She was also big on creating TikToks with her friends near and far. Outside of technology, she was your typical kid when it came to play, ranging from dolls, to stuffed animals, to a variety of aquatic games in the pool.

Play has a magical effect, at times, of taking away some of the stress and pressures of life. It is in these carefree moments that kids and adults develop and enhance certain skills that play a huge role in personal and professional development. I find myself reflecting on the seemingly endless positive impacts that play has on kids, yet it is being cut from schools everywhere. Ask any young kid what their favorite part of the school day is and chances are they will respond in no specific order: recess, gym, music, and art.

Our kids need and deserve more time for play in school. Recess is needed not just in elementary schools, but also during the middle and even high school years. In fact, in some ways, high school should be more like kindergarten than college. Play has to be valued in school and its integration should be a priority if student learning and achievement are the goal. Research has found that play develops students in four ways: physically, cognitively, socially, and emotionally. According to Ginsberg:

> *Play is integral to the academic environment. It ensures that the school setting attends to the social and emotional development of*

*children as well as their cognitive development. It has been shown to help children adjust to the school setting and even to enhance children's learning readiness, learning behaviors, and problem-solving skills. Social-emotional learning is best integrated with academic learning; it is concerning if some of the forces that enhance children's ability to learn are elevated at the expense of others. Play and unscheduled time that allow for peer interactions are important components of social-emotional learning.* (2017, pg. 183)

Play benefits students of all ages in four developmental ways while building thinking skills:

| Physical | Emotional | Social | Cognitive |
|----------|-----------|--------|-----------|
| Healthy and fit bodies | Empathy | Negotiation | Scientific thinking |
| | Persistence | Collaboration | |
| Agility | | | Inquiry and research skills |
| | Impulse control | Communication | |
| Coordination | | | Literacy skills |
| | Self-regulation | Conflict resolution | |
| Confidence | | | Independent, scientific, creative, and mathematical thinking |
| | Joy | | |
| Stress management | | Boundary setting | |
| | Resilience | | |
| | | Cooperation | |
| Large and fine motor skills | Self-confidence | | |
| | | | Language skills |

In order to create schools that work for kids, we need a concerted effort to break up the monotony of traditional learning practices that place a great deal of stress on students. Structured and unstructured play should be integrated into every school schedule, regardless of the age group served. Below are a few ideas to remember:

+ Add more recess time (kids need it and the benefits are clear).
+ Integrate makerspaces, a unique learning environment that encourages tinkering, play, and open-ended exploration for all (Fleming, 2017).
+ Replace study halls with play options and open choice activities.
+ Integrate games such as chess, checkers, Trivial Pursuit, and Xbox to common areas of the school.
+ Add time to lunch and encourage going outside or provide access to board games.
+ Develop a play-based elective course offering.

These are just a few ideas to implement play into the school day. Students should be excited to attend school and learn. By integrating more play, we can begin to create a culture in which more students want to learn. Once that is achieved, the possibilities are endless.

"Sticky" learning is just that—it sticks. If the goal is to empower students to think disruptively, then we need to use an array of strategies that create an experience that not only challenges students, but allows them to apply and process what has been learned in meaningful ways. While rigor and relevance represent focus areas to make this a reality, never forget the power of reflection, movement, and play.

DISRUPTIVE
CHALLENGE #4

Shadow a student during the school day to gain first-hand insight into what he or she experiences during a typical day. Reflect on the experience, noting, in particular, any "sticky learning" examples you observed. Select a sticky learning strategy (inquiry-based, performance tasks, reflection, movement, play) that is not regularly incorporated in your classroom or school. Develop an integration plan with criteria to measure success. Share an activity that was developed or implemented on social media using the #DistruptiveThink hashtag.

# PART 3:
## RE-THINKING THE LEARNER

# CHAPTER 5

# Adding a Personal Touch

*"Education is not the filling of a pail, but the lighting of a fire."*
William Butler Yeats

Education is at a crossroads. New technologies have radically changed the world in which we live and work across the globe. In many cases, this has been a good thing, but not always. Then came the COVID-19 pandemic, for which no one was prepared. The fact of the matter is that change isn't coming; it is banging on the door every day. The mantra of "that's the way we've always done it" is becoming less relevant with each passing day. As times change, many schools and districts are grappling with what to focus on in an effort to keep up with societal demands, a changing workforce, new areas of study, disruptive technologies, and learners who crave more relevant experiences. All kids doing the same thing, the same way, at the same time just doesn't cut it anymore. As a result, there is a need for a shift to a more personal approach to learning.

## Personalized Learning

How we best learn has been a hot topic for many years. Because there is no one-size-fits-all instructional model that works for all learners, there is no perfect answer to this question. Yet, learning experiences that are relevant, practical to our needs, meaningful, and applicable certainly contribute as factors that drive learning. The ability to acquire and construct new knowledge, then apply it in ways to solve complex problems, is at the heart of what education has been tasked with accomplishing. This lofty goal has fallen short of expectations as our education system has changed very little over the past one hundred years. As a result of the predominant one-size-fits-all approach to education, students enter an environment where their individual and unique needs are sometimes not met, resulting, in many cases, in unmotivated learners. Change is needed, and needed now, to better prepare learners for their future.

Although it is true that significant progress has been made in many areas of education, much more work remains. Thanks in large part to the work of Carol Ann Tomlinson (2016) regarding differentiated instruction, we have taken steps to design learning experiences for individual learners. In a nutshell, differentiation focuses on effective teaching strategies that provide students with different avenues to learn (often in the same classroom) in terms of: acquiring content; processing, constructing, or making sense of ideas; and developing teaching materials and assessment measures so that all students within a classroom can learn effectively.

Is differentiation enough and why has it not been incorporated at scale? Time might be one issue as well as a lack of resources to implement this approach consistently and with fidelity. Another factor is the apparent lack of focus on what students are really passionate about and aligning instruction to their learning interests. *Personalized learning* builds on the important foundation that differentiation provides by factoring in the individual

> Personalization represents a shift in focus from the "what" (content, curriculum, tests, programs, technology) to the "who" to create a more personal learning experience for all students.

interests and preferences of students aligned to their specific learning needs.

Personalization represents a shift in focus from the "what" (content, curriculum, tests, programs, technology) to the "who" to create a more personal learning experience for all students. At the forefront is developing and sustaining a culture that imparts purpose, meaning, relevance, ownership, and various paths that cater to both the learning strengths as well as needs of all students. It is critical to reach consensus as to what this then means in the context of teaching, learning, and leadership. Common vision, language, and expectations matter if the goal is to move beyond just a buzzword or isolated pockets of excellence. This shift results in a refined focus on the learner, including the following considerations:

- Knowledge and how it is used
- Authentic, relevant, real world contexts
- Building on diverse strengths/needs of all students
- Fostering independence and self-directed learning
- Ownership of learning
- Different ways to facilitate learning
- Use of tech to support and enhance learning

In education, each daily lesson can make or break a learner's experience in a classroom. Planning takes time. I remember many nights and weekends spending countless hours developing a variety of activities that would keep my students engaged while also following the scope and sequence of the curriculum based on the standards that needed to be addressed. As important as planning is, personalized learning is more about the experience than the lesson; however, the latter is necessary to create the former. The key to strengthening learning and instruction consists of the right balance of two main components:

1. Instruction (what the teacher does)
2. Learning (what the student does)

Balance surely is important. There is a time for direct instruction, but many learners would tell you that this component of a lesson is not what they really crave or find meaningful. Kids want a learning experience that is personal while educators try to ensure alignment with the very real expectations placed on schools across the world. Finding common ground in this area poses quite the challenge. Any personalization necessitates a move from "what" to "who" to emphasize ownership of learning. Sounds simple, but getting everyone on board becomes the challenge.

Success in this area requires a shared vision, language, and expectations that not only make sense, but also align with curriculum, standards, and assessment. Instilling a purpose of learning while challenging all learners in the learning process is at the heart of a more personal approach.

## 3 Shifts To Make Learning Personal

Solid instruction should lead to authentic learning experiences in which learners, themselves, are in the driver's seat. There are three critical shifts in practice that can lead to personal learning experiences for kids:

**Shift 1:** Are learners telling us what they know or showing that they actually understand?
**Shift 2:** Who is doing the work and thinking?
**Shift 3:** Who is asking or developing the questions?

There is obviously more to consider when embracing and implementing the shifts listed above. A personal learning experience doesn't sacrifice higher-level thinking and application just for the sake of relevance and meaning. Sound pedagogy provides the foundation with an added emphasis on scaffolding, innovative assessment, and improved feedback. Student agency and technology both play a huge role throughout by empowering learners through choice, voice, and advocacy. When these are combined to create effective blended learning activities in flexible spaces, the added elements of path, pace, and place further influence the personalization that will help kids flourish regardless of zip code or any label attached to them.

However, it is the third shift that tells the tale as to whether a lesson or task supports rigorous and relevant learning to create a more personal experience for kids. If kids see and understand the purpose of learning while being challenged, then they will ask more and better questions. Better outcomes rely on transforming teaching and learning practices in ways that engage, motivate, and inspire students. Making learning personal is a means to this end.

A more personalized approach to learning can result in increased relevance and value for students, leading to better outcomes and results. Advances in technology now allow educators to personalize learning through both blended and virtual pathways. For many students, these changes can definitely enhance and improve their learning experience. Personalized learning and technology do not represent a silver bullet for every problem within our current education system; however, when implemented correctly and appropriately, aligned to deeper learning outcomes, this approach *can* lead to deeper engagement and demonstration of what students know and can do.

## Student Agency

At New Milford High School, we were able to transform the learning culture of a traditional school and in the process achieve improved student outcomes while becoming an example that other schools emulated. This was achieved during a time of tumultuous change, as the education reform movement was just gaining steam. Even when challenges arose, we persevered as a school community thanks to a unified vision rooted in the fundamental belief that we could better serve our students in the future than we had in the past.

In a sense, all our major changes really started when we began involving our students in the process. This was also the reason, in my opinion, why change became sustainable. More often than not, change is orchestrated and directed at the adult level. There is often a great deal of talk about how many changes are being spearheaded for the betterment of students, but rarely are students themselves asked for their input or unique ideas. Schools need to work for our students, not the other way around.

> Schools need to work for our students, not the other way around.

If we are to improve learning and, ultimately, classroom-based outcomes, student agency should become a core component of the school culture. It's about empowering kids to own their learning (and school) through greater autonomy. It is driven by choice, voice, and advocacy. We learned a great deal about student agency during our school transformation process at New Milford including the following key elements of success:

- Develop pedagogically sound learning activities with standards-aligned assessments and allow students to select the right tool for the task to demonstrate conceptual mastery.
- Allow students to co-create rules and expectations.
- Create avenues for students to provide honest feedback on school culture. I held monthly meetings with all members of school government across all grade levels giving them an open forum to provide improvement ideas. Digital tools were used to continue the conversation. The key, however, was the follow-up on and implementation of some of the ideas suggested. Tools like *Mentimeter* can also be used to gather perception data from students.
- Implement portfolios as a means of authentic assessment.
- When hiring new teachers and administrators, include students on the interview committee.
- As policies that impact students are created or updated, provide a forum for kids to offer input.
- Integrate personalized and personal learning pathways such as

blended and virtual experiences.

+ Establish protocols for students to suggest new course and extra-curricular activity offerings.
+ Implement Academies or Smaller Learning Communities (SLC's), a school-within-a-school model.
+ Let students select books for independent reading based on their interests and reading level.

Meaningful change must begin with active student involvement. Advocacy, choice, and voice should occur in the classroom as well as throughout the school setting. Relevancy and value as perceived by our learners are central elements to success. Let's move away from catchy sound bites and clichés and begin to implement real strategies that will better prepare students for an ever-changing world.

## The Main Ingredients

To begin the move to personalization, it is important to understand all the interconnected elements, as depicted in the image on page 118:

### *Learning Environment*
The learning environment is central to personalized learning. The most important factor influencing this is the teacher-student relationship. It is also impacted by school culture and leadership decisions at both the administrator and teacher levels, such as policies, procedures, schedules, and facilities that treat all learners as unique individuals, including where and when kids learn. Technology can, in many cases, be a central component, but as I stated earlier, it is only an accelerator of learning, not the driver of learning. Some specific examples of learning environments that foster a more personalized approach include:

+ Flexible classrooms and spaces
+ Innovative schedules
+ No bells

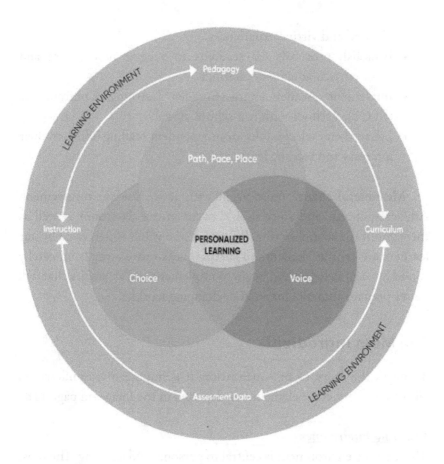

- Virtual courses or pathways
- Work-study and internship programs
- Academies and small learning communities
- Outdoor classrooms and spaces
- Field trips
- Bring Your Own Device (BYOD) and 1:1 devices
- Augmented and virtual reality

The key takeaway here is that personalized learning is much more than what happens in a classroom or the use of a tool. The right culture must be in place to create a learning environment conducive to unleashing the genius and talents of all students.

### *Curriculum*

Content knowledge is still essential across the board. *What* students are (and will be) learning matters, regardless of assertions by some pundits claiming otherwise. In some cases, the curriculum can be customized for learners to create a more personal experience. A more practical approach is to focus on specific strategies that help learners master content in ways beyond traditional methods. No matter the path taken, a rigorous and challenging curriculum is pivotal to successfully implementing and scaling personalized learning.

### Instruction

Instruction focuses on "what"—specifically, *what* the teacher is doing to effectuate learning. Strategies can include the simple ways in which we facilitate content such as modeling, explanation, and review. It centers around teacher actions as opposed to student learning. The key takeaway here is to ensure that the instructional strategies discussed in Chapter 3 are being implemented to impart a sense of relevance, purpose, and competence to the student.

### Pedagogy

Whereas instruction is "what" the teacher does, pedagogy is about the "how" and it more directly influences student learning. Pedagogy includes aspects of both the science and the art of teaching. It requires that teachers understand how kids learn and have the autonomy to design, implement, and assess activities that meet the needs of all students. Effective pedagogies, as discussed in Chapter 4, involve a range of techniques such as cooperative learning, guided and independent practice, differentiation, scaffolded questions and performance tasks, innovative assessment, and feedback. No matter the strategy selected, the goal is to develop higher-order thinking and metacognition through dialogue and relevant application.

### *Assessment Data*

Assessment determines *whether* learning occurred, *what* learning occurred, and *if* the learning relates to stated targets, standards, and objectives. Well-designed assessment sets clear expectations, establishes a reasonable workload (one that does not push students into rote reproductive approaches to study), provides opportunities for students to self-monitor, and provides educators with valuable data. Most schools and districts are proficient at collecting data through benchmark assessments and adaptive learning tools. Where the challenges and inconsistencies arise is how that data is analyzed and then used effectively to personalize learning. The following are starting points for better responding to the data we collect:

+ Grouping and regrouping
+ Targeted instruction
+ Differentiation
+ Tiered tasks
+ Re-assessment
+ Alternative options

The critical aspect here is to collect data, measuring what is valued, and then using it in ways to help students learn and grow, continuously closing the gap from where they are today to where they need to be next in order to reach their ultimate learning goals.

## *Voice*

Honoring students' voices and allowing them to have a say during the learning process is a central tenet of student agency. It can be defined as authentic student input or leadership in instruction, school structures, or education policies that can promote meaningful change in education systems, practice, and/or policy by empowering students as change agents, often working in partnership with adult educators (Benner et al., 2019).

In the classroom, it can be facilitated by posing questions or problems to solve and then allowing students to use digital tools to respond through text, video, audio, drawings, images, and gifs. Having every student respond on an individual whiteboard and then holding their board up for the teacher to see is a non-tech example. In many cases, voice can be amplified through the cover of anonymity, which is critical for introverts and shy students. They can also be provided with opportunities to share opinions on classroom design, assessments, and feedback. Student voice includes any act that empowers a student or students to make their voices heard when shaping their learning experiences. The main takeaway here is that everyone is involved in the classroom and feels more a part of the experience.

### *Choice*

Choice might be one of the most uncomplicated components of personalized learning. Choice can come in the form of kids selecting the right tool for the right task to demonstrate thinking, choosing where to sit in a classroom with flexible seating, or deciding how much time to spend watching a flipped lesson. It can also manifest itself in blended learning models such as must-do/may do menus, choice boards, and playlists, which will be discussed later in this chapter. At one school where I served, we even allowed students the choice of swapping out a face-to-face class we offered in the building for a virtual course that we didn't offer.

### *Path, Pace, Place*

If all kids are doing the same thing the same way at the same time, individual needs are not being met. Just throwing technology into the mix isn't a pedagogical solution. I will say this again. Putting all kids on a device to use an adaptive learning tool and calling it personalized learning is actually counterproductive to personalizing student learning. The three P's of Path, Pace, and Place provide added flexibility to emphasize a more personal approach to learning by allowing kids to follow their own *path* at their own *pace* while being afforded the optimal *place* in which to learn.

Path can come in the form of customized curriculum, asynchronous virtual courses, selecting the order in a playlist, or independent study. It allows students to progress towards standards based on their mastery levels, interests, and goals. In my former school, students were able to determine their individual paths to learn something new through our Independent Open Courseware Study (IOCS) program (bit.ly/IOCSNMHS). Pace is as simple as allowing kids to work through activities, self-managing their time in order to achieve mastery. In many cases, a timeframe is established in the classroom as students work through activities in a variety of blended learning models. Some kids need more time, others less. Place refers to where kids learn and can include flexible seating, hallways, outdoors, home, or virtual spaces.

The image below highlights key aspects of the five core elements to promote student agency:

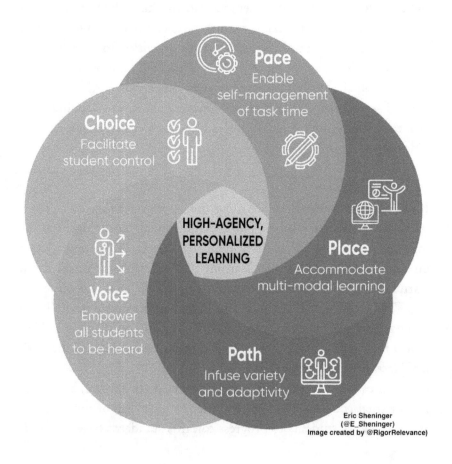

Eric Sheninger
(@E_Sheninger)
Image created by @RigorRelevance)

Like many things in education, organizations and people tend to make concepts more complicated than they really are or they craft a vision and definition that solely meets their needs or goals, not those of students. Personalized learning is about meeting individual student needs and building off the strengths and interests of individual learners. It is also a way to ensure equity, because all students will be getting what they need, when and where they need it to succeed.

## Blended Pedagogies as a Way to Personalize

I remember back in 2012 when we began to implement blended learning strategies at my former school. At the time, the flipped approach to instruction was popular and best suited for the resources we had and the age group of our students. The goal was to make the learning experience more personal for our students while better meeting their individual needs in the process. In our case, this meant using time more efficiently during the school day to transfer the balance of power from instruction (teacher-centered) to learning (student-centered). A great deal has changed since 2012 when it comes to blended learning. As technology has evolved, so have many of the opportunities inherent in this strategy.

With the right conditions in place, blended learning is one of many strategies that can add a level of personalization for students. However, there seems to be a bit of confusion as to what blended learning is or the conditions that must be established for it to improve feedback, differentiate instruction, and empower learners. The majority of what educators are calling blended learning is actually blended instruction. The difference is subtle, but important. Blended instruction is what the teacher does with technology. Blended learning occurs when students use technology to exert control over the path, place, and pace of their learning.

For me at least, the distinction above brings a great deal of context to the discussion of how technology can improve learning for our students. It is not necessarily bad practice when educators merely integrate digital tools into their instruction. As long as questioning focuses on higher levels of knowledge, students can show what they understand using digital tools and that's a good thing. However, this is not blended learning. If students genuinely own their learning, then they must have some level of control over path, place, and pace while receiving more personalized feedback regarding standard mastery and concept attainment.

The significant shift that we should focus on is what the student is purposefully doing with the technology provided. Student agency is at the heart of effective blended learning. It is also important that it supports high-level learning, provides better means of assessment, and improves feedback. Blended instruction is a start, but blended learning is much more impactful.

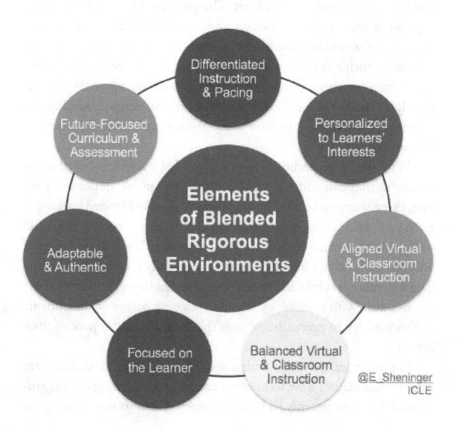

When working with educators on blended learning, we always focus first and foremost on ensuring that sound pedagogical design serves as a foundation for everything to follow. Essential pedagogy—including strategies, elements, models, and supports (tools)—must be prioritized for blended learning to flourish.

Effective instructional strategies that are widely accepted when it comes to sound pedagogy will always be a foundational component. As you either create or evaluate blended activities, are these included in some form or another? If not, think about where there is opportunity for growth. When moving from whole group teaching to blended learning think about how the strategies discussed in previous chapters can be incorporated as part of small-group instruction while the rest of the class is engaged in other activities. The value of checks for understanding, targeted support through differentiation, feedback, and assessment can all be amplified.

The real power of pedagogically-sound blended activities is to empower kids to take more ownership over their learning while making the experience more personal in school. Many of these elements require increasing student agency (choice, voice, path, pace, place), incorporating flexible learning environments, and creating tasks that involve the purposeful use of technology to collaborate, communicate, and create. You will also notice that some are interchangeable. For example, many quality blended activities allow students a certain level of choice over their learning path. Keep in mind that one element might support or enhance another.

There are many personalized learning models available that can be used effectively as well as many different strategies for educators to choose from. In theory, these sound great but implementing them into practice is an entirely different animal. Some of the most popular models I see being used with a high level of efficacy in schools include:

+ Station rotation
+ Choice boards
+ Playlists
+ Flipped approach

With station rotation, students are grouped based on data and move through a variety of set activities typically consisting of targeted instruction with the teacher, collaborative exercises, independent work, and online tasks that are personalized for individual learners. The teacher establishes a block of time for each station and students visit each one during a class period followed by some sort of formative assessment. Groups are dynamic, not static, changing periodically determined by ongoing assessments and data analysis. A ready to use template can be found at: bit.ly/SRtemp

Choice boards allow students to select a set number of activities to complete from numerous options. In many cases, there are nine tasks of which three must be completed. However, a teacher could also develop assignments that all students must complete followed by a set number of choices to complete when finished. No matter the option used, it is important to scaffold and differentiate the tasks and upon completion have each learner complete a formative assessment activity. When developing a choice board considering the following:

+ Use pre-made templates that can be created or acquired through a Google search. For some examples visit: bit.ly/CBtemplates
+ Use a timer for pacing and self-management.
+ Behind the scenes, the teacher works with students needing targeted assistance.
+ Add links to your Learning Management System (Google Classroom, Canvas, Schoology, Microsoft Teams, etc.) to see student work and to hold them accountable.
+ Monitor regularly to ensure on-task behavior.
+ Create a scaffolded formative assessment for all students to complete once they are finished (three questions or more that increase in difficulty).
+ If students finish the required choices and formative assessment, have them choose other activities to complete.
+ Consider using Google Slides and adding either anchor charts or essential content for review to assist with completing the board.

Playlists are relatively easy to implement. After whole group instruction, the teacher develops a series of individualized assignments that students work through at their own pace while following the path of their choice. The time period for this varies, but it is typically over a few days. As students complete a task, they either color in the corresponding box on a digital sheet next to their name or check off each box on a paper worksheet. While the majority of the class progresses through the playlist, the teacher can work one-on-one with students who need the most assistance. Unlike a choice board, students complete all tasks in a playlist. The following guidelines outline some best practices for creating effective learning playlists:

+ Provide direct instruction prior to introducing new content either through a mini-lesson or flipped approach.
+ List tasks in a learning management system (Canvas, Schoology, Google Classroom) and use a Google Sheet for students to color in once a task has been completed. In cases where digital equity is an issue, these can be listed on paper for distribution, while any activities involving technology would need to be replaced.
+ Scaffold questions and activities to increase the level of thinking required.
+ Build in relevant problem-solving opportunities to instill greater purpose while providing appropriate challenges.
+ Use data to determine the need for one-on-one or small group support.
+ Ensure there is a balance between tech and non-tech options.
+ Integrate adaptive tools that respond to student strengths and weaknesses while providing data that can be used for groupings and instructional shifts.
+ If possible, differentiate by providing multiple versions that address the specific needs of learners while providing different pathways for learning.
+ Create a simple formative assessment for learners to complete after they have finished all activities in the playlist. This could

consist simply of three scaffolded questions. Not only does this provide closure, but it will also provide insight as to whether students engaged in all the tasks.

Flipped lessons are ones in which students watch a short direct instruction video or consume other forms of content outside of school at their own pace while communicating with peers and teachers using online tools. While in school, students work to actively apply what they have learned through concept engagement and empowering learning activities with assistance from the teacher. Flipped lessons allow teachers to become facilitators of learning, moving away from the "sage on the stage" approach to instruction. A goal of the flipped learning model is to maximize the amount of time spent on learning while actually in the classroom.

There is no shortage of tools available that can be used as part of the models listed above when a sound pedagogical foundation is in place. The key is not to get caught up in the blended *instruction* piece and, instead, to keep moving towards blended *learning*. A list of popular tools I have seen used effectively that is updated regularly can be accessed at bit.ly/edtechdisrupt. These are all fantastic options that can be aligned with the strategies listed above. When it comes to differentiation and summative assessment, I recommend the integration of adaptive learning tools. Yes, there is a cost to these. However, learners can be pushed based on ability level and the data gleaned can be used during small groups to provide targeted instruction.

## Blended Learning in the Classroom

One day I was conducting some learning walks with the administrative team at an elementary school outside Houston, Texas as part of longitudinal work that spanned three years. Throughout each school year, our work focused on digital pedagogy as it related to blended learning and the use of flexible spaces. The primary goal was to take a critical lens to instructional design with a focus to set the stage for disruptive thinking. I cannot overstate the importance of first getting the instructional design right before throwing technology into the mix.

A secondary goal was facilitating a transition from blended instruction to blended learning. As mentioned previously, this is not to say that the former is ineffective, depending on whether the technology is merely a direct substitute for traditional low-level tasks. The dynamic combination of pedagogically-sound blended learning and choice in either seating or moving around in flexible spaces results in an environment where all kids can flourish and want to learn.

Over the course of my time working with educators at the school, I saw much growth and improvement to the point that we began seeing the future of education in the present moment. Unlike our learning walks during the beginning phase of the work, teachers at the school did not know I was going to be in the building on this particular day. The idea was to see if the goals for digital pedagogy and blended learning were being accomplished.

During the learning walks, we consistently observed students actively engaged in meaningful learning. In one 4th-grade classroom, we saw a Tic Tac Toe grid displayed on the interactive whiteboard. It is a method of offering students choices in the type of products they complete to demonstrate their knowledge. As in a traditional Tic-Tac-Toe game, students are presented with a nine-cell table of options. The teacher should make sure that all options address the key concept being learned. There are several variations on this method: 1. Students choose three product options that form a horizontal, vertical, or diagonal line. 2. Students choose one product choice from each row or from each column (without forming a straight line). 3. The teacher can create two or more versions to address the different readiness levels.

This activity incorporates choice, formative assessment, purposeful use of technology, and differentiation. In this particular classroom's version, all learners had to complete the middle box with the gold star emoji. Flame icons represented activities that were more difficult. You can see an image of this choice board and many others in the resource link at the end of the book.

It is important to remember that technology need only be a small component of an effective blended learning activity when considering the strategies, elements, and models described earlier in this chapter. In this example, only three of the nine choices involved technology. Autonomy was emphasized to better democratize the experience. Learners explored and demonstrated high levels of understanding related to concepts while constructing new knowledge. As for the technology component, it's what the kids do with tech to learn in ways that they couldn't without it. Blended learning makes this a reality.

I was so focused on the structure of the lesson and the engagement of the learners that I almost missed what possibly could have been the best part of the class—an opportunity to reflect. Once learners completed the choice board, they had to respond to the following prompts:

- Today I did well at _____.
- I did well because _____.
- After today I need to work on _____.
- I will do this by _____.

It is important to understand the convergence of so many elements present in the examples above that align with sound instructional design and real blended learning. Learners had a certain amount of control over path, pace, and place thanks to using flex spaces and the Tic Tac Toe activity that incorporated blended elements. This is a hallmark of a well-structured blended learning activity, as is choice, flex seating, and voice, each of which was also present in the learning we observed.

Over the course of my time working at the school, I have seen countless similar examples of exemplary blended learning activities implemented by teachers across all grade levels. As fabulous as the teachers at the school have been in implementing transformational learning experiences for their students, this could not have occurred without the vision and support of an outstanding administrative team in place at the school. They provided unwavering support to their teachers while also learning alongside them. When an entire school believes in doing things differently, takes collective action, grows together throughout the process, and collects evidence to show improvement, the result is efficacy in action.

## Personalization in Action

While working with another district on their personalized learning initiative, I saw first-hand how job-embedded, on-going, and targeted support leads to amazing changes in practice. On one occasion, a few district administrators and I visited several classrooms. We saw some solid examples of station rotation, but overall, there was a great deal of room for growth in terms of personalizing student learning.

The district office later arranged for me to facilitate a two-hour workshop that focused on the key elements and structures of personalized learning addressed in this chapter. After the session, a team of second-grade teachers stayed behind to begin planning how to implement what they had learned. Several more months passed before I once again had the opportunity to visit classrooms throughout the school. We noticed significant growth across all classrooms, but the second-grade team stood out as exceptional in terms of what each was doing. We saw personalization in every classroom.

In some cases, you could see teachers had co-planned while others went down their own path. We saw learners grouped by ability, accessing choice boards digitally on their iPads once specified tasks were completed. Teachers were even able to monitor progress in Apple Keynote and push kids to other tasks if they stayed on one choice too long. When finished with a task, students dragged an "X" over it. In other cases, learners submitted video and audio evidence through Keynote in both ELA and math. Another teacher had essential questions mapped out for the entire week and daily reflections where kids supplied evidence of what they learned. Voice was honored through the effective use of Nearpod during a whole-group lesson.

As I continued to process what I saw, I figured it would be best to capture from each teacher why they decided to change, how they specifically changed, and what results they have seen from these changes. Here are their reflections:

### Ranell Whitaker

*Our 2nd-grade team was so excited about the first visit you had at Snow Horse Elementary. You had some pictures of choice boards that you showed us during your presentation that really inspired me. I had been doing Daily 5 in my classroom for several years with a very rigid schedule and exact assignments that every student was to complete within their 15-minute time frame. I felt that it was going OK, but I never felt like there was enough time for me to work with a small group or one-on-one with students. The students were also frustrated because some weren't able to finish assignments within the given time, and some students had too much time, and either didn't know what to work on or started to distract and disrupt others.*

*I looked at the choice boards you showed us and knew we could implement something similar. The night of your presentation, I went home and created my own choice boards for the next day for math and language arts, and we started implementing them the very next day. My students LOVED choosing what activity they would work on, and when they would work on it. I noticed the students were more engaged and excited about what they were doing because they had a CHOICE! And best of all, I stopped hearing, "Teacher, what should I do now?"*

*I did start with a more structured approach to the choice boards, and each student had a printed-out version to cross off the items they completed. After several weeks of trial and error on choice board activities, I now feel that the students have exciting activities and games that help them excel and achieve their goals, all while they are choosing activities that challenge them. The activities include reteach, extra practice, and enrichment. I have also allowed students to use the amount of time they need for their activities with no problems. When they finish one activity, they are excited to start on a new choice.*

*Just about a month ago, we decided to go digital with the choice boards using Keynote. It was a game-changer. Students are now able to have their choice boards right on their iPads and show their work by uploading photos of their work or inserting a screenshot right on the choice board. I send them a new choice board for the week each Monday, and then on Friday they airdrop it back to me or send it via Apple Classroom. I am no longer making a million copies of worksheets and choice boards for the kids to turn in. They turn in one choice board at the end of the week, and I can see exactly what they accomplished in the time that they were given. If I notice a student has not completed much on their choice board, I am able to pull them aside and talk about how they are using their time and how they can improve. If a student is picking the same choice each day, I can speak to them and challenge them to try something new. I am also easily able to assign students specific choices as a "must do" if I feel it necessary.*

*Overall, this change has really opened me up to work with each child in my classroom EVERYDAY. I can pull a group as needed, and the students that I pull can get right back to what they were doing when they finish working with me. I am not trying to cram as much as I can into their brains in fifteen minutes, and students can spend as much time as they need on a task (which they want to finish so that they can move on to the next activity they choose). I also don't feel the pressure of a time constraint as I did with timed rotations. I am thrilled with the choices my students make to challenge themselves and am so happy with the growth and progress that they have shown in the last few months. My students have learned the joy in accomplishing a task and have gained a lot of responsibility and accountability in their own education.*

## Jonna Sutterfield

*When you came to visit back in the fall, what you had to say was exciting, and frankly, I just believed in it. It was eye-opening to think, yes students can make their own choices in how they want to learn, and more importantly, it opened up avenues to let students explain their learning at their level. It has given confidence to my students to be able to show me their way of understanding. That day struck a chord with my team and me, and we were so excited to implement personalized learning.*

*Today you saw how our Math usually goes. The students started out where I wanted them on their own levels. For example, a small group challenge problem with a must-do task to perform. Once they completed that, they were then off to their own Digital Choice Boards to complete activities on their own. Within the Math Choice Boards are a variety of activities from which they can choose. They know where to find more challenging stuff, extra practice, and games, etc. to further their learning. For the most part, students will always be choosing wisely, and at times I feel I need to encourage some to try something new or others just to make choices!*

*Their choice boards are all digital, and they have them on their iPad. They do a daily check-off, and on Fridays, send them back to me. I do a quick check (I usually know what they are doing daily). So, it is more of a double-check. I don't grade them, except for participation. These choices are for them to implement what we are learning in class on their own and practice that.*

*My number one thing that I take away from personalized learning, that I share with others, is how much it has opened me up to meeting the needs of my students. I have been able to pull small groups daily to reteach or even check for understanding. I love that I can immediately see their learning right then and there. They are roaming and trying new things and learning how to work on their own and sometimes with partners. With me being more accessible, I love that more of my students' learning goals are being reached, and I have a greater understanding of their learning, which helps me find more ways to challenge them and encourage them to try something new.*

*Also, the students are more engaged in what they are doing, and Math Choice and Daily 5 Choice are some of their favorite times. They get excited to move around and do a variety of learning.*

### Erin Fuller

*I absolutely love my math choice boards. After we jumped in and made our first-choice board, it was amazing to me how much the students loved choosing how they learn. I also love how it frees me up to help each child, either by challenging or reteaching them.*

*During my math block on Monday, we started a new chapter on 3-digit addition. To begin my block, I always do an explicit lesson by starting with* the essential question. I use Keynote to make my math choice board. The first slide states the essential questions for the entire week. The second slide is the actual choice board that they work off of each day. The third slide is the most important one for me. This is where they show me what they know each day. I either have them video themselves explaining the concept or do an audio recording answering a question from the lesson.

On the choice board, the middle row includes the things that the students must do each day. I want them to practice fluency, do independent practice, and ten minutes in our differentiated math program each day. On the top and the bottom rows, I have built-in choices that they can use to take their learning to a higher personal level. I have put X's, checkmarks, and picture place holders on this slide, so they can show me what they're doing to learn during the week. If there is something that I want a specific student to do, I will circle it on their board to let them know I'm looking forward to seeing that completed. I changed it to a weekly board rather than daily, so they can only do one activity a week instead of spending every day doing the same thing. I have worked hard to challenge certain kids with activities to enrich them as well as activities to help fill in gaps with others. Another thing I love is where they can check off if they worked with me because I needed them to or if they chose to get extra help on their own.

The last slide is so informative to me. I can quickly see if they get it by having them answer specific questions for me. This is the most valuable part to me because I can see which child gets it and which child doesn't immediately. If I am worried about them before the end of the week, I just grab their iPad and listen to the video they made that day, and I can give immediate feedback. This is also helpful if I need to talk to a parent about a concern. It is also beneficial to have when a parent tells me that their child is bored and isn't being challenged. I can show them their choice board and talk about how they are choosing not to challenge themselves.

My choice boards, not just math but also my Daily 5 Choice boards, have changed my teaching. I know where my students are, and I know what they're doing to learn. This frees me up so that I can work one-on-one or in small groups on what they need, not just what I think they need after a full *group lesson. Previously, I had never been able to immediately tell where each of my students was academically.*

### Jana Vanhorn

*Today in my classroom, I created a Nearpod for my students. This week we are reading about different regions in the world, and I wanted to build some background knowledge before we started reading stories. The Nearpod included virtual field trips, open-ended questions, drawing pictures, and more. I have found that during a typical classroom discussion, I get the same students who participate and the same students who "check out." My students LOVE learning through Nearpod. They are more likely to be engaged in the learning and I get a response from every student. As a teacher, I have found that it is so valuable to get a response from every student because there is usually at least one or two who don't understand what to do or how to answer a question. I can now quickly have a conversation with them to get them back on track.*

Whether personalizing pedagogical strategies or instructional techniques, these teachers illustrate how implementing innovative approaches can have a positive impact not only on student learning, but also on their own professional practice. These teachers took some information provided to them and charted their own course forward. You might even say they experienced personalized learning themselves.

Many learners have suffered from inequity because of socioeconomic status, inefficient resources, or ineffective pedagogy. If all kids are doing the same thing, at the same time, the same way, and in the same place, it raises a red flag. The time is now to do something about this. Equity is about providing each learner what he or she needs when and where they need it in order to succeed. Disruptive thinking requires us to disrupt our practice in the classroom for more equitable and enhanced student outcomes. Authentic personalized learning can make this happen.

DISRUPTIVE CHALLENGE #5

Create a personalized learning experience either for students in your classroom or the educators you support. Choose from either station rotation, choice board, playlist, or flipped lesson/faculty meeting. The key is to select something you have not implemented before. Make sure at least two elements of agency and scaffolding are included. Share an image or a link to your task on social media using the #DisruptiveThink hashtag.

# CHAPTER 6

# Environments That Cultivate Thinking

*"Given a rich environment, learning becomes like the air—
it's in and around us."*
Sandra Dodd

A constantly changing world compels us to look at societal trends as inspirational elements and potential catalysts for change in the structure of our classrooms as well as the designs of programs in both physical and virtual spaces. It is a call to action challenging schools and educators to critically reflect on the environments that should embody a learning culture. Do they meet the needs of today's learners? Do they foster and inspire creativity, provide flexible opportunities to learn, and address unique and specific interests? Are they reminiscent of what students will expect in today's world as well as the future? We must look past traditional constructs and begin to incorporate trends embraced by innovative Fortune 500 companies to transform where and when kids learn. When we invest energy and time answering these questions, our classrooms will become better equipped to authentically empower students, preparing them for success today and tomorrow.

Improved thinking environments require us to act. It is our individual and, more importantly, collective actions that will help us to move from "what has always been" to "what can possibly be" in terms of where learning occurs. As you begin to develop action plans for your classroom or school that tackle both large and small changes to learning environments, pause to think deeply on the process involved. The process of change results in action, but there are many key elements that must be considered to ensure that these actions prove successful. Consider current obstacles and challenges as you navigate the change process to transform learning for all students.

Talk, opinions, and assumptions about learning environments might be interesting, but they quickly lose their luster without substantive actions to accompany them. Examine ideas and strategies you are exposed to with a discerning eye. Think about where and when you learn best. Then ask a few questions to help establish a plan for action:

- How will this improve teaching and learning?
- Is the idea or strategy scalable?
- How will it benefit learners?
- What research and evidence exists to support the proposed action steps?

Don't get sucked into the rabbit hole of fluff. Just because something looks good on Pinterest or sounds great on Twitter does not mean it is an effective practice. Always pause to reflect on anything you are exposed to, whether from a conference, workshop, keynote presentation, book, article, video, blog, tweet, or any other source. We have

> Just because something looks good on Pinterest or sounds great on Twitter does not mean it is an effective practice.

isolated pockets of excellence in schools across the world when it comes to learning environments that empower kids to think disruptively, but pockets of excellence are not enough; every child deserves such excellence. If we want to prepare our students for the world in which they will live, work, learn, play, and connect, the time to act is now.

## Using Research to Drive Change

Research should be used to inform as well as influence the actions we take to implement sustainable change at scale, whether it is in a classroom, school, or district. It also helps to move those who are resistant to embracing new ideas. One area that represents a growing body of research is learning space design. In studying various pieces of literature on the effect of design, Barrett and Zhang (2009) began with the understanding that a "bright, warm, quiet, safe, clean, comfortable, and healthy environment is an important component of successful teaching and learning" (p. 2). Their research found direct connections between the learning space and sensory stimuli among students. The evidence of such connections came from the medical understanding of how human sensory perception affects cognitive calculations. As such, Barrett and Zang (2009) identify three key design principles:

1. **Naturalness:** Hardwired into our brains, humans have the basic need for air, light, and safety. We must consider the impact of lighting, sound, temperature, and air quality on learning.
2. **Individualization:** As individuals, each of our brains is uniquely organized and we perceive the world in different ways. Because of this, different people respond to environmental stimuli in various ways. Therefore, the opportunity for some level of choice affects success.
3. **Appropriate Level of Stimulation:** The learning space can offer the "invisible curriculum" that affects student engagement levels. When designing the space, it's important for educators

not to overstimulate and thus detract from students' ability to focus, but to provide enough stimuli to enhance the learning experience.

Supporting this notion, a research study out of the University of Salford Manchester (UK), followed 3,766 students in 153 elementary classrooms from 27 different schools over a three-year period, analyzing classroom design elements along the way. The report found clear evidence that "well-designed primary schools boost children's academic performance in reading, writing, and math" (Barrett, Zhang, Davies, & Barrett, 2015, p. 3). The study found a 16 percent variation in learning progress due to the physical characteristics of the classroom. Additionally, the study indicated that whole-school factors (e.g., size, play facilities, hallways) do not have nearly the level of impact as the individual classroom.

Educators may dismiss the notion of redesigning learning spaces due to financial constraints. However, research indicates that you don't need to spend vast amounts of money to make instructional improvements. In fact, changes can be made that have little to no cost yet make a significant difference. Examples include altering the classroom layout, designing classroom displays differently, and choosing new wall colors (Barrett et al., 2015). These research-based factors requiring minimal financial commitments can help boost student outcomes.

The effect of learning spaces on various behaviors—territoriality, crowding, situational and personal space—has been the focus of sociological and environmental behavioral research. The consensus of this research is that the space itself has physical, social, and psychological effects on individuals within the space. One study measured the impact of classroom design on twelve active learning practices, including collaboration, focus, opportunity to engage, physical movement, and stimulation (Scott-Webber, Strickland, & Kapitula, 2014). Research findings indicated that designing learner-centered spaces provides for more effective teaching and learning. In this particular study, all major findings supported a highly positive and statistically significant effect of active learning classrooms on student engagement.

In a research study examining the link between standing desks and academic engagement, researchers observed nearly 300 children in 2nd through 4th grade over the course of a school year (Dornhecker, Blake, Benden, Zhao, & Wendel, 2015). The study found that students who used standing desks exhibited higher rates of engagement in the classroom than did their counterparts seated in traditional desks. Standing desks are raised desks that have stools nearby, enabling students to choose whether to sit or stand during class. The initial studies showed 12 percent greater on-task engagement in classrooms with standing desks, which equated to an extra seven minutes per hour, on average, of engaged learning time.

It is clear that creating flexible spaces for physical activity positively supports learning outcomes. However, it is not simply the physical layout of the room that affects achievement. One particular study investigated whether classroom displays that were irrelevant to ongoing instruction could affect students' ability to maintain focused attention during instruction and learn the lesson content. Researchers placed kindergarten children in a controlled classroom space for six introductory science lessons, and then experimentally manipulated the visual environment in the room. The findings indicated that students were more distracted when the walls were highly decorated and spent more time off task. In these environments, students demonstrated smaller learning gains than in cases where the decorations were removed (Fisher, Godwin, & Seltman, 2014).

Design can empower learning in amazing ways. Understanding how the space itself can affect the way students learn is key. However, we must make sure it is done the right way. Decisions about learning space design must be made by the people who are actually working in classrooms. Teachers need to either have a seat at the table when making such decisions or actively advocate for support and autonomy to make changes to classroom design themselves.

## Design that Empowers Thinkers

All one has to do is look around and see the amazing changes that are taking place in workspaces across the world to imagine how we can redesign our schools and classrooms. I have always been enamored with what Google and Pixar have done to improve working conditions for their employees. The unconventional workspaces they have created support the notion that a creative environment helps stimulate minds and inspire innovation. Gone are the boring white walls. In their place are graphical wallpapers and dry-erase surfaces. Some have even completed a total overhaul of the office layout, designing a unique, collaborative working ecosystem with the end goal of inspiring each individual and team to work more effectively and efficiently, laying the groundwork for innovative ideas. Incorporating design elements that foster creativity, collaboration, flexibility, and communication have allowed for increased productivity. As expectations related to producing better outcomes change, businesses have capitalized on a design trend that has led to improved results.

Now let's take a look at our schools and classrooms. What do they look like? Do they look similar to the classrooms and schools you attended many years ago? This is not a trick question, but a stark reminder of an issue that needs more attention. Do kids really want to sit at uncomfortable desks aligned in rows with loads of artificial light? If you think so, then I challenge you to take the place of a student not just for a day, but an entire week. Sit in that uncomfortable chair until your back and neck are aching and then ask yourself why we do this to kids. Design issues extend well beyond that of the classroom, however. The internal structure of most schools does very little to reflect living and working in the world outside the schoolhouse walls.

Change in design can improve student learning. A study by Barrett et al. (2012) puts this into perspective. The yearlong study by the University of Salford's School of the Built Environment and British architecture firm Nightingale Associates examined 751 students in 34 classrooms across seven primary schools for the 2011-2012 academic year. Students were assessed at the beginning and end of the year for academic performance in math, reading, and writing, and classrooms were rated on environmental qualities like classroom orientation, natural light, acoustics, temperature, air quality, and color. Researchers

> Leadership is about action, not title, position, or power.

found that classroom architecture and design significantly affected academic performance: Environmental factors affected 73 percent of the changes in student scores.

These findings also suggested that the design of a classroom could have a 25% impact (positive of negative) on a student's academic performance. Armed with this information, educators are in a strong position to advocate for resources to create classroom and school environments that are much more conducive to learning. If the messaging falls on deaf ears, think about what you can do on your own. The key point here is to become a champion for change regardless of your role. Leadership is about action, not title, position, or power.

A trip to Google's New York City office really put things into perspective for me. I was fortunate to attend a Chromebook training session with my students back before the device entered the market at scale. While engaging in professional learning throughout the day, we had an opportunity to explore the facility a bit as we moved between sessions and lunch. I had heard many rumors about life at Google and discovered that most of them were true.

Scooters were used as a means of transportation. There were even racks throughout each floor for Google employees to park their scooters. There was a Lego wall in a lounge area where bins of different sized and colored pieces catered to the imagination. It was clear that employees are encouraged to unleash their creativity when it suited them. The Angry Birds and super-sized Ferris wheel designs I saw were quite impressive.

Specialized areas and rooms were located on every floor. Two that stood out were the gaming and massage rooms. Mini-kitchens were everywhere. It was obvious that nutrition was a priority at Google. Some of these kitchens were decorated in particular themes. One of the most elaborate mini-kitchens I saw was decorated as a jungle complete with hammock-like chairs, small waterfalls, decorated trees, and live frogs. Equally impressive were the massive espresso, cappuccino, and coffee machines in each kitchen as well as the overwhelming number of food and beverage options available to employees.

Google-themed artwork was visible throughout the building. Company pride was apparent everywhere. Clever reminders not to do certain things were visible on doors and windows. One sign throughout the building was a picture of an alligator with its tail propping the door open. Each picture was accompanied with this reminder, "Beware the Tailgator!" Obviously, Google didn't want certain doors propped open for security reasons. Office spaces where entire walls were whiteboards created the perfect conditions for brainstorming and outlining creative ideas. These offices also included large tables that could seat 12-16 people.

I felt like I was in a dream. Open spaces were outfitted with collaborative and comfortable furniture (leather couches, plush lounge chairs) not to mention more coffee stations. An extensive bistro dining area provided employees with an unparalleled lunch experience. The chef preparing a special of the day was a nice touch, as well.

Today's educational paradigm is no longer one of knowledge transfer but one of knowledge creation and curation. The "cells and bells" school environment model has been prevalent for more than a century, but it is no longer relevant for today's learners—or today's educators. As educators work to shift to instructional pedagogies that are relational, authentic, dynamic, and—at times—chaotic in their schools, learning spaces must be re-evaluated and adapted. Pedagogical innovation requires innovative design changes to the spaces in which learning takes place. Simply put, if the space doesn't match the desired learning pedagogy, then it will hinder student learning outcomes.

## Flexibility is Critical

Do you remember the classrooms that you learned in as a child? I sure do and not for positive reasons. Each room was a carbon copy of another, where you would have many uncomfortable desks lined up in neat little rows. The exceptions were my science classrooms, which were outfitted with lab tables instead of rows of desks. However, there was still the issue of sitting in chairs for long periods of time that strained our backs. Uncomfortable seating options and a lack of movement led not only to discomfort, but it also had a negative impact on engagement. Of course, some lessons were extremely engaging. However, the conditions under which learning was supposed to take place were not conducive to the process at all. Little did we know at the time that classroom design could be different. It was what we always knew and came to expect and never thought twice about it.

The evolving research on the importance of classroom design and routine movement has begun to challenge the status quo in terms of the classroom and school learning environments. Some positive changes are being implemented in schools. For example, typical classrooms with desks in rows are now a thing of the past in some schools. They have been replaced by more contemporary furniture that is not only comfortable but also modular. Flexibility, choice, and movement are all being incorporated to make the school experience more enjoyable while setting the stage for increased engagement and collaboration. The key is to create the same learning conditions for our students that we, as adults, would want to learn in ourselves.

Although such changes to the physical environment of schools and classrooms can seem exciting, here is a critical question to keep

> **Flexible spaces must lead to flexible learning.**

in mind: As learning spaces change, does pedagogy change as well? In some cases, the answer is yes; in others, the answer, unfortunately, is no. If kids are comfortable while receiving direct instruction or all completing the same activity at the same time, then what's the point of new furniture or updated spaces? As the saying goes, if you put lipstick on a pig, it's still a pig. As precious funds are used to upgrade classrooms and entire schools, improvements to learning must be at the forefront of our planning. Flexible spaces must lead to flexible learning. Here are some questions to pose when considering learning environment redesign:

- How will it support more movement and application of knowledge or competencies?
- How will it promote higher levels of student agency?
- How will pedagogy change in ways that lead to more personalized approaches?
- How will assessment and feedback change or improve?
- What will be the role of technology?
- What professional learning support is needed to maximize the use of flexible environments?

If you have already invested in flexible seating, think about the questions above in terms of what has changed. One strategy that addresses all the questions I pose is a move towards pedagogically-sound blended learning, discussed in Chapter 5. It is important not to confuse this with the use of technology to support or enhance instruction.

The three "P's"--Path, Pace, Place--ensure that flexible environments live up to both the hype and potential to improve learning for kids. In my work with schools on implementing blended learning to maximize the investment in innovative environments, I typically showcase several models that I have found to be most effective. These include (as mentioned previously) station rotation, choice boards, playlists, and flipped lessons.

Educators are now inundated with ideas on how to better design classrooms and schools. It is always prudent to analyze both the work and the investments that are made to determine if there are improvements to learning and school culture. It is OK to be skeptical of what you might see shared on social media when it comes to learning spaces (or anything else, for that matter). We need to move away from classroom design that is "Pinterest pretty" and use research, design thinking, and innovative pedagogy to guide the work. The space will not improve outcomes on its own. It's how the space is used in ways that better prepare learners for now and in the future that will.

## Remote Environments

The COVID-19 pandemic shifted the focus from physical to remote learning environments overnight and has set the stage for more virtual class offerings in the future. One of the most prominent obstacles encountered during this chaotic and seismic shift in how we facilitate learning experiences for our students was getting and keeping kids engaged in the learning. Engagement begins with a focus on sound instructional design that leads to pedagogical techniques that foster active learning. A balance between digital and non-digital activities is preferred, but you might have to lean one way or another depending on the availability of technology and WiFi in your respective community. No matter the situation, the key to empowering learners is to create valuable and meaningful experiences that they want to engage in every day. Below are six areas to consider when developing any type of remote learning activity for maximum student engagement:

### *Relevance*
Without relevance, learning simply does not make sense to many students, as noted in Chapter 3. The "why" matters more than ever in the context of remote learning. What one must do is step into the shoes of a student. If he or she does not truly understand *why* they are learning what is being taught, the chances of engagement and improving outcomes diminish significantly.

### Discourse

Social isolation is a real issue impacting many kids who learn virtually. There is a dire need for students to interact with their peers, especially during synchronous lessons facilitated through live video tools. Discourse can easily be achieved through the purposeful use of technology. If kids are just consuming content and completing activities in isolation, then chances are many will be disengaged.

### Collaboration

Another way to counteract social isolation and potential social-emotional issues is through collaborative experiences. These leverage the power of discourse while students work together to solve a problem or complete a performance task. Using the elements of well-structured cooperative learning (accountability, timeframe, equitable roles, equal opportunity to participate) activities can be designed as part of a remote blended learning experience. In the end, it is about creating the conditions for positive interdependence, group processing, and interpersonal skills.

### Flexibility

Rigid schedules and expectations didn't work particularly well prior to COVID-19. Not surprisingly, they don't facilitate an engaging learning experience for kids in a post-COVID-19 world either. Having kids meet at the same time for a synchronous Zoom session as they would for a traditional face-to-face class just doesn't make sense and is counterproductive. Any successful remote learning implementation ensures that flexibility is a core component in both attending lessons and completing work. Asynchronous workflows that are set up with some content can lead to higher engagement if there is some flexibility aligned to getting assignments done over a specified timeframe.

### Personalization

Many of the areas I have already discussed are integrated throughout a personalized experience. It represents a shift in focus from the "what" (content, curriculum, tests, programs, technology) to the "who" to create a more personal learning experience for all students. At the forefront is developing and sustaining a culture that imparts purpose, meaning, relevance, ownership, and various paths that cater to all students' strengths and weaknesses as detailed in Chapter 5.

## Engagement Leads to Empowerment

There is a pressing need to develop and implement pedagogically-sound strategies that work in a remote environment for virtual learning to be successful. I remember facilitating three intensive virtual workshop days with educators from a school district in Pennsylvania. They were a fantastic group to work with virtually. The dialogue, openness to new ideas, and willingness to take risks was apparent each day. What made it even better was how much I learned from the experience.

One of the main challenges with remote learning has and will always be student engagement. As I planned out my activities for the three days, I really wanted to create a meaningful experience that included numerous opportunities for discourse and collaboration. Using Zoom breakout rooms and an array of digital tools, we were able to schedule significant time for interacting. When designing lessons for remote learners, here are some tips based on what I learned:

- Establish behavior and participation norms.
- Mute everyone during synchronous instruction to start. I have found this to be extremely beneficial in setting the tone for attentive behavior.
- Have an interactive activity ready to go every 10 – 15 minutes.
- Add the question prompt or task in the chat box (I just copy and paste it from my slide deck).
- Unmute everyone and then place them randomly into breakout rooms.
- Provide regular updates to students by broadcasting messages to all rooms.

+ Remind students that there is an "ask for help" button. This is a great way to combat cyberbullying or to respond to group questions.
+ Jump into rooms to monitor activity and provide support.
+ Upon closing the breakout rooms, mute the entire class again.
+ Provide a digital tool for all kids to share their responses to the question discussed or task completed.
+ Encourage ongoing dialogue and questions using the chat box.
+ Encourage the use of earbuds or headsets if you are managing both face-to-face and remote learners at the same time.

## Remote Learning Collaboration Strategies

VIRTUAL BREAKOUT ROOMS

Think -Pair-Share

Turn and Talk

Jigsaw

Station Rotation

Brainstorming

padlet

Eric Sheninger (@E_Sheninger) / Image created by @RigorRelevance)

Collaboration during synchronous lessons is crucial to keeping kids engaged. It also sets the stage for structured cooperative learning activities that could occur live or asynchronously as part of remote blended learning. It is essential to be intentional about planning for discourse and collaboration in any remote learning lesson or experience, just like we would in a face-to-face setting. Students desperately need interaction with their peers to create some sense of normalcy while increasing attentive behavior and engagement in the learning process.

In order to empower people, you first need to engage them. It is nearly impossible to create a culture of learning if elements of boredom, inactivity, and irrelevance are present. This is a lesson I learned as a presenter and workshop facilitator. Early on, I used more traditional strategies since this was a new arena for me. The shift from principal to full-time consultant brought a certain amount of fear. Thus, I reverted back to what I was comfortable with in terms of what I could control and what I perceived that educators wanted. I basically became a master of direct instruction with little participant interaction.

I thought I was doing a pretty good job because no one told me otherwise. There was consistent eye contact and the feedback I received from surveys was mostly positive. It wasn't until a presentation at a major conference where I got the kick in the butt that I desperately needed but wasn't aware I deserved until then. As I was reading Tweets from the session, a participant basically told me that I spoke at them the entire time and didn't provide ample opportunities for greater discourse, practical application, or reflection.

It was at this point years ago where I began to embrace and model the very same strategies that were being used at my high school when I was a principal. I included multiple opportunities for discourse and collaboration as well as time to develop action steps. Engagement was amplified with a focus on the how, with exemplars from all types of schools and the use of digital tools to provide everyone with an opportunity to respond using their voice. In essence, my role is now more of a facilitator of learning than a deliverer of knowledge. Another key change was intentionally developing ways to personalize the experience for those with whom I am fortunate to work.

These changes, combined with what I hope is a unique style grounded in relationships, have enabled me to better connect with educators. I greatly benefitted from these changes in the remote and hybrid world we all experienced in some way. As someone who supports educators all over the world in this area, it is critical that I not only engage as many people as possible, but also model the most effective strategies that could be implemented in the classroom. We get what we model.

The pandemic created countless issues for educators to address, with engagement being at the top of the list. We can and should learn from this and get better, because no one knows what the future holds. Whether you are face-to-face, remote, hybrid, or are integrating virtual classes keep these strategies in mind:

+ Begin each lesson with an anticipatory set to get kids excited and impart relevance.
+ Call on students who have their camera and microphone off. By consistently setting expectations in this way, the stage will be set for increased attention and participation.
+ Integrate breakout rooms for discourse and randomly pop into them.
+ Use Google or Canvas forms to conduct quick checks for understanding (1-3 questions max) throughout the lesson.
+ Leverage digital tools for voice and choice. It is also a good practice to use these following any breakout room activity to get a grasp on engagement levels.
+ Evaluate the level of relevance in questions, tasks, and assessments.
+ Develop means for accountability through routine feedback and timely grading.
+ Include closure at the end of each lesson or synchronous session.
+ Move to tasks and work that are more purposeful through blended strategies such as station rotation, choice boards, playlists, self-paced activities, and flipped approaches.
+ Assign less work while diving more deeply into important concepts.

Engagement is grounded in a learner's sense about why they are learning something and how it will be used in their personal life. It can be achieved through a combination of context and application. Think about what motivated you as a learner and what still does today. This might be the best starting point of all to set the stage for thinking about engagement in remote environments. If kids aren't engaged during the instructional component, then it is quite difficult to empower them later on, regardless of whether they are offline or online. Technology plays a huge role, which is why all efforts need to be made to eliminate the digital divide.

## Avoiding Learner Burnout

The COVID-19 pandemic resulted in some monumental shifts to teaching and learning practices. Educators have reflected as to why they teach the way they do and how it can be done more effectively. For virtually every school that implemented some sort of remote or hybrid learning model, you can bet that video conference tools played an enormous role. While it is helpful for educators to now have a variety of tool options at their disposal post-pandemic, there is a growing concern that must be addressed if learning is the goal.

Have you heard of Zoom fatigue? It is a real thing, I assure you, and it applies to Microsoft Teams, Google Meet, or any similar platform. Facilitating professional learning using video conferencing tools is exhausting.

I bet many of you have experienced the same thing in meetings and professional development during the global pandemic. Now we need to see ourselves in our learners' shoes to provide experiences that both engage and empower them. It becomes harder to do this if we miss the mark with the synchronous component. Kids experience Zoom fatigue, just like adults. It's a real phenomenon that results in mental, physical, and emotional exhaustion.

Below are some strategies to consider in order to gain maximum impact from any live video tool:

- Interactivity during synchronous sessions in the form of discourse and collaboration is vital, as is being laser-focused in terms of the content to be delivered.

- Less is more in this case, and brevity combined with sound instructional design can work to create impactful lessons.
- Co-create norms with learners for behavior, attentiveness, and interaction.
- Begin with a short anticipatory set to infuse relevancy and get learners fired up about the lesson or activity.
- Infuse routine breaks that incorporate movement and social-emotional (SEL) activities.
- Achieve a balance through the use of asynchronous learning tasks detailed later in this chapter that can empower learners both on and off screen. Authentic challenge problems always work well.
- Try to keep the direct instruction component between 10 - 15 minutes with at least two checks for understanding to break up adult talking.
- Bookend the synchronous component of the lesson with ten minutes in the beginning to review prior learning and ten at the end for closure.
- Seek feedback from learners and families on how they feel about synchronous video lessons.
- Build-in time to reflect on whether the synchronous component of the lesson was successful. Ask yourself, "Would I have been engaged and empowered if I had been the learner?"

Fatigue is yet another challenge that educators need to overcome as more virtual learning options are provided to students. Most of us know all too well how this feels, which compels us to act. A healthy combination of sound pedagogy, professional learning support, feedback, and reflection will help any educator grow and improve their craft.

## Asynchronous Learning

Asynchronous learning provides flexibility that better meets the needs of both students and teachers by relinquishing the familiar rigidity of school. It also supports both independent and collaborative work when structured the right way while supporting critical competencies such as self-management, creativity, inquiry, and teamwork. There can also be a mix and match of both digital and non-digital activities that allow students to actively apply what has been learned in relevant and meaningful ways. To get started, consider these tips:

+ Determine how content will be disseminated (synchronous or asynchronous).
+ Map out activities in alignment with standards.
+ Establish learning targets.
+ Determine how much time students will have to complete the tasks.
+ Consider developing scaffolded formative assessments for students to complete after a series of asynchronous activities as a form of closure and to check for understanding.
+ Provide a few assessment options and allow students to select which one is graded.

There are many practical strategies for developing asynchronous tasks. Keep in mind that some rely on technology, while others do not. With self-paced activities, the possibilities are endless, including independent reading with reflective questions, scaffolded question sets, inquiry or problem-based performance tasks, or virtual pathways. In the case of the latter, students can work through self-paced content and courses on Khan Academy. Another great resource to incorporate self-paced activities is CK-12 (www.ck12.org). Be sure to click the "explore" tab on the top toolbar and check out the adaptive practice, simulations, and interactive games that can all be completed in a student-controlled format.

Giving students a choice as to the activities in which they engage is a simple way to empower them to learn while providing enhanced learner ownership. Choice boards, introduced in Chapter 5, represent a solid blended learning strategy where tasks can be scaffolded, differentiated, and contain a mix of digital and non-digital options. To get started, view examples that can be accessed through a simple Internet search or take what you have already created to the next level. Choice might be one of the most simplistic high-agency approaches to integrate into daily lesson planning. If creating a board is not your thing, simply start with "must do" and "may do" activities. Sometimes flexibility can be as simple as letting kids pick the order of the tasks during asynchronous learning. Unlike choice boards, playlist or menu activities are completed by a student at their own pace as detailed in Chapter 5. Be sure there is a balance between individual work and collaborative tasks using digital tools, enabling kids to connect with their peers.

Nothing replaces sound instructional design and pedagogy, but adaptive technologies have a great deal of potential to support and advance thinking skills. In a nutshell, adaptive technologies use computer algorithms to orchestrate interaction with the learner and deliver customized resources and learning activities to address each learner's unique needs. These powerful tools can help close achievement gaps and limit learning loss as part of a teacher's asynchronous arsenal of strategies and supports.

If there was ever a time to try a flipped lesson, that time is now. This strategy is not new by any means and can easily be adapted to a remote environment. Teachers can record their direct instruction component of the lesson in short clips, typically 10 - 15 minutes. Concepts can be explained using mini whiteboards, slide decks, or digital tools like *Educreations*. These can then be uploaded to your learning management system (LMS), such as Google Classroom, Schoology, or Canvas. If you don't currently use one of these, no worries—the videos can be added to a class Google Site. After watching the video at a preferred pace, students then complete a series of asynchronous activities to construct new knowledge and apply what was learned from the content presented.

A major benefit of asynchronous learning activities is their inherent flexibility, which can be a benefit to students, educators, and parents alike. Tasks and assignments can be completed over a specific time period using strategies addressed in this book as well as more traditional options such as research papers or projects. They can also free up the teacher to work with those learners who most need targeted instruction or extra help.

## Celebrate Small Wins

Largely as a result of COVID-19, educators have now had time to absorb and adjust to a new reality. Now is the time to embrace the upside of this moment, let go of some of the old baggage and self-imposed limitations around what we think school really *is*, and expand our idea of what teaching and learning *can become*. Creative, asynchronous learning opportunities are a vital way to ensure that learning remains dynamic, impactful, and even more equitable. It seems like every day presents a new challenge or adventure, depending on how you view the current landscape. There are no easy answers or solutions that will work for everyone.

We must not discount even the smallest successes during both good and trying times; doing so is a simple and authentic way to build people up and maintain momentum. Over time these small wins can morph into catalysts for more extensive change efforts. During workshops and coaching sessions, I am always asked what advice I have to help teachers and administrators make things as easy as possible while ensuring quality learning is taking place. In this case, the goal is trying to achieve more systematic change that all educators can embrace. The bottom line is that it must make sense and not require a great deal of effort to implement.

Below are the three recommendations to help educators persevere in a rapidly changing world. These can serve as a foundation for virtual, as well as physical, environments as we move forward regardless of any obstacle that lies ahead. They are relatively straightforward, but each requires a certain level of continuity and consistency. I tend to refer to these as norms that everyone can get behind:

1. Embrace a systemwide learning management system (LMS).
2. Settle on a video conference platform with breakout rooms.

3. Use one digital tool designed to increase engagement and promote empowerment.

The consistent use of an LMS such as Google Classroom, Schoology, or Canvas works to create a more equitable learning environment for all kids and families provided there is access in school and at home. It can become the hub for all lessons, videos, activities, assessments, and student work. A foundation can then be established for more personalized approaches such as pedagogically-sound blended learning or self-paced activities. Students and families win because they have on-demand access to resources. Building capacity now benefits all educators through vertical articulation and provides a foundation to build upon in subsequent years. If a student is sick or on homebound instruction he or she won't miss a beat.

Many schools relied on a video conference platform for synchronous instruction and learning during the pandemic. Like the LMS, consistent use across a district or school helps develop continuity, especially in upper-grade levels. For discourse and collaboration, selecting a video conference platform that has breakout room capability is a must. No matter the platform selected, it is crucial to follow guidelines to protect student identity and information.

There are many digital tools available to educators these days, which often creates an overwhelming feeling. It's not how many tools you use that matters, but instead, the degree to which they are employed to facilitate engaging and empowering experiences. Hence, my advice is to master one tool first and use it consistently to review prior learning, check for understanding, and provide closure. The key here is establishing a comfort level among both teachers and students. There are many great tools out there to use. My advice is to pick one that allows for student responses to be used in different ways. Two to consider are *Mentimeter* and *Padlet*.

The success of each suggestion above hinges upon providing or seeking out professional learning support for using the tool or platform, as well as sound pedagogy. This represents a great starting point to help educators manage expectations and create an environment conducive to thinking. The recommendations can set the stage for more structured experiences that empower learners in different ways. They can also be a springboard for future change.

## Changing Environments Require New Competencies

It seems as if we are always in the midst of difficult times. The world was fundamentally changed during the pandemic and the challenges that were placed on society go without saying. In classrooms, educators grappled with the impacts this had on both remote and hybrid learning models. It wasn't easy, and many people were at a breaking point, and who could blame them?

As the dust settled, we learned critical lessons. The world of work has fundamentally changed and continues to change with each passing day. A necessary shift emerged right before our eyes. More and more employers moved away from physical spaces and embraced remote environments while placing greater levels of trust in their employees. What this equates to is less focus on the number of hours put into a day and more focus on getting the work done at a high level of proficiency.

Reporting to an office or being required to put in a set number of hours each day doesn't necessarily result in success. So, what does this mean for education? A greater emphasis on productivity in the future of work will require our learners to have a refined set of competencies. It is important not to get caught up in the hoopla about needed "skills." While these are important, they focus on the "what" in terms of the abilities a learner needs to perform a specific task or activity. Competencies outline "how" goals and objectives will be accomplished. While Chapter 4 outlined six specifics that will always have value, now and in the future, our learners will most likely need to be competent in the following areas to succeed:

- **Self-regulation:** Process by which people plan for a task, monitor performance, and reflect on the outcome.
- **Remote collaboration:** People work together, regardless of their geographic location, to achieve organizational goals using a variety of digital tools.
- **Critical thinking and problem-solving:** The ability to think in complex ways and apply knowledge and skills acquired in relevant ways. Even when confronted with perplexing unknowns, people are able to use extensive knowledge and skills to create solutions and take action that further develops their skills and knowledge.
- **Emotional intelligence** (EI): A person's capacity to be aware of, control, express one's emotions and handle interpersonal relationships judiciously and empathetically. A person who is competent in EI can understand, manage, and use their own emotions to communicate effectively, relieve stress, empathize with others, overcome challenges, and defuse conflict in positive ways.
- **Time management:** Process of organizing and planning how to divide the time you have available between specific activities or delegate tasks to others depending on organizational structure. In a nutshell, it's about working smarter, not harder, to achieve goals.
- **Creativity:** The ability to develop and successfully implement innovative solutions to complex problems while connecting seemingly unrelated phenomena.

Moving forward, educators must develop their own sense of what is most critical for the learners they serve. The curriculum might dictate *what* has to be taught, but the art of teaching is all about *how* we teach in ways that inspire meaningful learning. As the world continues to change in ways that we could never have imagined, it is imperative that learners have what they need to succeed today, and in the future. Their environment will have a dramatic impact on their thinking. We must improve physical school and classroom spaces but look beyond them as only one place in which kids can learn. The pandemic resulted in an experiment in remote learning at a grand scale. It might not have been smooth sailing, but we learned powerful lessons along the way. Chances are that schools of the present and future will now be more open to remote learning and it is imperative that all educators are fully-prepared for that distinct possibility.

DISRUPTIVE CHALLENGE #6

Visit at least five different (physical or virtual) classrooms together with five colleagues noting the environment in particular. Reflect on the visits, sharing thoughts about what features enhanced learning as well as any features of the environment that inhibited learning. Based on the experience and takeaways, develop three specific actions that can be taken to improve the learning environment in your own setting. Share an image on social media that illustrates your findings and tag it with the #DisruptiveThink hashtag.

# PART 4:
## RE-THINKING OUR MINDSET

# CHAPTER 7

# Outlier Practices

*"Normality is a paved road: It's comfortable to walk,*
*but no flowers grow on it."*

Vincent Van Gogh

A s a kid, my parents used to take me to professional baseball and hockey games all the time. Even though I was an avid sports fan, I think I looked forward to the food and walking around the venue more than watching the sport that was being played. Over time this changed, but as a kid, eating junk food all day and not worrying about calories, sugar, or fat was the life. Herein lies my point. I vividly remember the food and atmosphere, but not the score of each game. The same can be said for a variety of other experiences that have shaped my life and influenced my thinking over the years.

Almost all of us have heard the phrase, "Experience is the best teacher." Growing up, I heard it a great deal. At the time, I didn't appreciate it or fully understand its meaning, but now I wholeheartedly concur. Of course, there are some experiences I wish I could have avoided that resulted in negative outcomes, but they are still a significant component of my story. The driving force behind the decisions we make are the innate beliefs we have about ourselves. Our experiences, both positive and negative, shape who we are. They become an integral part of us and create our story.

When it comes to school, what do students remember? In the short term, it might be grades. However, as the years pass, any grades earned become a distant memory. I don't remember any of my marks from K-12, but I do know that I was an above-average student. What stands out most vividly in my memory are the amazing experiences that some of my teachers provided me in their classes.

Mrs. Williams had us draw pictures in Kindergarten that depicted what we wanted to be when we grew up. At the time, I wanted to be a farmer. In art, Mr. Wynn was one of the coolest teachers I ever had. Since I went to a K-8 school, I had him as a teacher for nine years. Even though I was a horrible artist, he was always able to provide some sort of positive reinforcement. Mr. South had us evaluate how we would colonize Mars as 7th graders and then create prototypes of inventions that would help us get there as described in Chapter 4. Dr. Hynoski used humor and showed compassion in high school chemistry and anatomy. I struggled to earn a good grade in both classes, but because of the classroom culture he created, I worked hard. I never had Mrs. McDonald or Mrs. O'Neil as teachers, but they were both student government advisors who were always willing to lend an open ear, whether related to school or personal issues.

These teachers—and a handful of others throughout my own K-12 educational journey—engaged in practices that were memorable and perhaps even outside the norm. They did not focus on grades and homework; instead, they focused on learning and creating experiences designed to enhance students' learning and push our thinking. In many ways, they were "outlier" educators who engaged in "outlier" practices which resulted in outside-the-box thinking and learning on the part of the students with whom they interacted. Pockets of excellence such as these examples are no longer good enough. Now is the time for all educators to adopt outlier practices in many areas, including grading, homework, and feedback practices.

## Thinking Beyond Grades

The teachers above, and many more, helped to mold me into the person I am today, not because of their grading practices, but through the fantastic experiences they created for my classmates and me. Although grades might work for some students, they are counterproductive to the learning of many others, including those who:

+ Feel ashamed by the stigma that a letter or number has (or had) on them.
+ Do not learn in the one particular way that their class is structured.
+ Receive high marks without really trying or without being challenged and thus walk away questioning what was really learned.
+ Are punished through unfair grading practices such as zeros, where their final grade doesn't adequately reflect what they learned.
+ Find no relevance and meaning during their time in a particular class or course.

The key takeaway here is that more often than not, it's the engaging, relevant, meaningful, fun, awe-inspiring, practical, and empathetic experiences that kids will remember long after they have had a specific teacher or graduated from a school. The result is the formation of relationships that serve students better than any letter or number ever will. These realizations set the stage for thinking differently about grades. For grades to really mean something, there must be a deeper, more emotional connection beyond what is just seen on a report card or transcript. This is when authentic learning occurs.

For centuries, school success has been largely determined by grades as the main reflection of what students do—or do not—know. What has resulted is a rat race of sorts where many kids and parents alike have their "eyes on the prize." The "prize" in this case is either a coveted letter or number grade that is celebrated above the most important aspect of education—whether a student actually learned and can apply this newly constructed knowledge in meaningful ways. Micro-credentials and digital badges, although a step in a better direction as a means to making feedback more personal, can also perpetuate this problem.

The process of grading is convoluted and fraught with errors and arbitrary decisions. Just think about the inherent issues with traditional points systems. Many grades are determined using an accumulation of points over a set amount of time including homework (often, just checked for completeness), extra-credit, meeting (or failing to meet) behavioral expectations, participation, or a loss of points for late assignments. The problematic issues relating to traditional grading practices are not new. After an analysis of several research studies, Alfie Kohn (2011) concluded the following:

+ Grades tend to diminish students' interest in whatever they're learning.
+ Grades create a preference for the easiest possible task.
+ Grades tend to reduce the quality of students' thinking.

Grading perpetuates a bigger problem. If students come through our doors each day to just get a grade, then we have already failed them. By failure, I mean a disregard for providing them with the necessary competencies and qualities that a grade can rarely quantify. Unfortunately, in most schools today, grading remains a major component of the school experience, compelling kids to go through the motions and "do" school, earning a high grade as their reward. We have (inadvertently, perhaps) motivated our students to subordinate learning in favor of grades in their quest for school success. Learning, not grades, should be the reward students seek. Helping them recognize this is a challenge we must all accept. The learning pit concept discussed in Chapter 4 has always resonated with me. With learning as not only the goal, but also the final outcome, students are guided through a process that illustrates how learning is the ultimate reward for their efforts. When grades are thrown into the mix, the focus becomes a path of least resistance, negating the positive outcomes associated with students experiencing the learning pit.

What is the hard truth about traditional grades and how they are currently used? Truthfully, I think grades are more for parents and schools than they are for the students we are trying to serve. Learning is not only a messy process, but the path also varies greatly from student to student. All kids think and learn differently and possess different and unique abilities to show us that they understand concepts. Inquiry-based projects and performance tasks that students engage in are a great example of this point. Through learning experiences such as these, students learn through trial and error, failure, collaboration, cross-disciplinary connections, taking risks, and overcoming certain fears inherent in traditional grades. The ultimate reward is making something that does something, in many cases, discovering a workable solution to a problem they identified.

I fear we are a long way off from abolishing grades altogether in our schools, but that does not mean we can't critically reflect on the role grades play and how they are calculated while continuing to advocate for change. If the true goal of school is disruptive thinking that leads to deep learning, then that should be reflected somehow in a grade. We must begin by developing better formative and summative assessments that move away from students telling us what they know and instead showing us that they understand. We also need a mindset shift, encouraging students to work and think in ways that allow them to experience the inherent rewards of entering and exiting the learning pit.

## Re-Thinking Zeros

The dreaded zero. For many students, this number elicits a certain amount of fear and anxiety when it comes to their grades. I, for one, felt this way and made sure that everything was turned in when it was due. Compliance and following rules, even if I didn't agree with them, were just natural parts of how I viewed (and "did") school. Unfortunately, not all students viewed school as I did and not all students are as compliant as I was. Sometimes they forget. Other times they just don't care. Regardless of the reasons, I think it is essential to critically examine the message and lesson that we are imparting to our youth through this outdated and, quite frankly, insensitive grading practice.

The practice of giving zeros to students who do not turn in assignments when they are due has pretty much been entrenched in schools across the world. It is one of many examples that fall into what I call the "death trap" mantra of education: "That's the way we have always done it." Just because something has been done in the past, or is a traditional component of school culture, does not mean it is an effective practice. In my opinion, it is well beyond the time to revisit this practice and determine if it truly is in the best interests of our learners. Consider the scenario below:

*Isabella is an engaged learner who always pays attention in class, has a high class rank, and has never made a grade lower than an A. Her first four grades in physics are 100, 99, 99, and 98. Isabella is set to have a 99 average for the term. However, she has had an unusually busy week with cheerleading, and when she arrives at school on the morning the final assignment is due, she realizes that she has completely forgotten to do it. She explains her situation to the teacher and begs to be allowed to turn it in the next day. The teacher is unsympathetic and assigns Isabella a grade of zero for the final assignment, telling her that this will prepare her for the "real world."*

Let's examine the last statement regarding preparation for the real world. Correct me if I am wrong, but in education, teachers and administrators don't receive zeros if they:

+ Arrive to work late.
+ Fail to meet a determined deadline (e.g., turn in lesson plans, complete all observations/evaluations by a set date).

- Ignore an email and, as a result, are unprepared for meetings or don't get needed information to colleagues when required.
- Forget to call parents back.

We should not doom a colleague to failure for behaving in any of the above manners, yet that is what we do to the kids we serve when they are given zeros. The question becomes what message or lesson are we really teaching students through this practice? The "zero" has an undeserved and devastating effect on students and their grade—so much that no matter what the student does thereafter, the "zero" distorts the final grade as a true indicator of mastery (Wormeli, 2006). Grades aside, it tells us absolutely nothing about whether a learner can think. If learning and growth is the goal, then it is our responsibility to tackle this issue because the negative impacts on our learners far outweigh the need to make an example or fall back on the "preparation for the real-world" rationale.

As a principal, I worked with our staff to tackle this issue, as well as the overall practice of grading. I'm not going to lie; it was one of the hardest change initiatives I ever engaged in during my tenure as principal. Our eventual solution was not perfect or even the best example by any means; however, it did represent a step in a better direction because we began focusing more on learning than on grades. Through examining research and arriving at consensus, we revamped our grading philosophy. Here is where we landed in regard to zeros and why:

**No zeros**: Students are not assigned a grade of zero (0). This practice not only reflects grading as punishment but also creates a hole from which students cannot dig out (Guskey, 2000; Reeves, 2004; Reeves, 2008; O'Connor and Wormeli, 2011). This includes homework, quizzes, tests, projects, etc. An exception to this would be cases that involve cheating, plagiarism, or a midterm/final exam absence without a justifiable excuse ( e.g., doctor's note, death in the family).

Again, this was by no means a perfect solution, but, for us, it was a small step in the right direction as we began prioritizing learning over grading. My hope is that any educator reading this book works with their school community to enact grading changes that work for them—and, more importantly, their students. Instead of assigning zeros, consider marking the work as incomplete until it is turned in. It is important to determine why students don't turn in specific assignments such as homework and projects as a way to mitigate even having to consider doling out zeros. Reflect on the following questions:

+ Is the assignment meaningful and relevant?
+ Does the learner see the purpose in it?
+ Will feedback be provided?

Reflecting on these questions can help lead to the creation of better assignments that are more relevant and that kids actually *want* to complete. Punishing learners with zeros destroys both motivation and a love of learning. They also paint a false picture of what was actually learned. If a grade does not reflect learning, then what is the point? We owe it to our students to pave a better path forward when it comes to assessing their learning.

## Feedback Cultivates Thinking

The most successful companies become successful by always looking for ways to improve. When it comes to their employees, there is no ceiling, as they are continually pursuing pathways and allocating resources to help the best get even better. The same philosophy can be applied to our classrooms. Continuous feedback for all learners, regardless of their innate abilities or their current performance level, is critical if the goal is to help them become the best they can be. Extensive research has shown that feedback is one of the most effective classroom practices impacting student learning (Goodwin & Miller, 2012).

The bottom line here is that feedback matters in the context of learning. It should also be noted how it differs from assessment. Feedback justifies a grade, establishes criteria for improvement, provides motivation for the next assessment, reinforces good work, and serves as a catalyst for reflection. As mentioned previously, the valid assessments determine *whether* learning occurred, *what* learning occurred, and *if* the learning relates to stated targets, standards, and objectives. In reality, formative assessment is an advanced form of feedback.

In my opinion, you can never provide learners with too much feedback. However, the way in which it is delivered matters significantly. Nicol (2010) found that feedback is valuable when it is received, understood, and acted on. How students analyze, discuss, and act on feedback is as important as the quality of the feedback itself. I have identified the following five components of effective feedback:

1. Positive delivery
2. Practical and specific
3. Timeliness
4. Consistency
5. Using the right medium

Although providing effective feedback to learners is critical, it can also be time consuming. How can educators realistically provide learners with quality feedback during every lesson? The answer lies in sharing the responsibility with them. I often observe teachers monitoring students during collaborative learning activities or working with specific groups face-to-face in blended learning station rotations. During debriefs, I often ask how feedback is given. Often, the response is that feedback is presented verbally. This is a necessary strategy at times, but more is needed. This is why I came up with the idea of feedback logs.

Think about all the conversations that educators have with learners on a daily basis. The valuable information in many cases aligns with what the research has said constitutes effective feedback. The problem, though, is the reasonable possibility that learners forget what they have been told regarding progress or improvement and they don't have the ability to later reflect on the feedback that was provided. You know how the saying goes: Out of sight, out of mind. Having students create a feedback log solves this issue by helping them remember, retain, reflect upon, and chart their progress. Best of all, it requires no extra time on the part of the teacher.

A feedback log can be created in many ways and aligned to competencies, concepts, or standards. Students can then use this as a means to track their progress and growth over time as additional feedback is provided over the course of the year. If students genuinely own their learning, then they must be put in a position to reflect and then act on the feedback they are given. The use of a log can also strengthen partnerships with parents. By making them aware of the log, parents have an opportunity to be more involved in their child's learning each day.

Implementing feedback logs as a part of consistent professional practice saves precious time, can be seamlessly aligned with research-based strategies, will help students monitor their understanding of essential learnings, and can be used to provide more targeted support to those students who don't show expected growth over time. They can also serve as an empowerment tool to help students exert more ownership over their learning.

It is also important to understand our role in providing feedback. No one relishes the opportunity to be talked at incessantly, regardless of their age. Even though there are most certainly cases that necessitate this, context matters. I often think about how we give feedback to our learners, colleagues, and those we supervise. Maybe "give" is the wrong word to use here. The prevailing notion is that one person speaks while the other(s) listens intently and reflects on the advice given. Herein lies one of the greatest misconceptions about an effective feedback loop. In many cases, feedback is seen as something that is "given" to another person. It becomes even more complicated when it is viewed as something that must be "delivered."

When there is an emphasis on delivery, we run the risk of focusing more on what is said as opposed to a process that fosters reflection and, ultimately, clarifying questions from the receiver. Often, we settle on what the feedback is in terms of what people have or have not done well from our perspective. So much time is then given to mapping out the feedback that we want to share with the other person that it becomes more about us than the person or people we are trying to help. When done in this manner, it can be construed as criticism rather than a catalyst for growth.

If the purpose is to help others grow, then a mentality of delivering the message or advice must be rethought. Feedback should be a dialogue, not a monologue. A conversational approach can lead to high value and actual changes in practice. Below are some specific reasons why the conversation is such an integral part of the feedback loop:

- The receiver sees that it is more about him/her than the giver.
- Imparts a greater sense of trust on behalf of the receiver, resulting in a more powerful relationship with the giver.
- Creates the space for open reflection based on what was shared.
- Opens the door for discussion about potential action steps to be taken.
- Provides the receiver with an opportunity to present his/her own perspective on the feedback provided. This can result in the sharing of evidence or more context that the giver might not have been aware of when initially providing the feedback.
- A conversational approach can motivate people to seek out feedback.

Delivering feedback in the form of a monologue is an outdated process that can be improved whether you are working with kids or adults. Instead of preparing how you are going to "deliver" the message, think about creating the conditions for optimizing how the receiver will value the feedback. A conversation that incorporates the art of listening will go a long way to creating a classroom and school culture in which feedback is not only sought and invited, but acted upon.

## The Value of Homework

I have so many fond memories of my childhood. Growing up in a relatively rural area of Northwestern New Jersey sure had its benefits. As we returned home from school each day, my brothers and I would jump off the bus and diligently make our way about a half-mile to our house. Once home, we would peel off the backpacks, get changed, and play outside for the remainder of the day until dinner was ready. I can still remember my parents yelling into the great abyss, as many times we were either deep in the woods or down by the local farm. There was homework, but it was very manageable to the point that my mom had to remind me that we actually had some during our elementary and middle years.

When not off on adventures in the deep woods, we would be riding bikes, playing with the dog, swimming in the pool, shooting hoops, or getting into some kind of trouble. Life sure was fun and relatively stress free. Things changed a bit once Atari and Nintendo took hold. Most of our time was still dedicated to outdoor play, but time was also now allocated to playing these wonderful video games. On some days we couldn't wait to get home from school to play Asteroids, Pac Man, Donkey Kong, Tecmo Bowl, and Mike Tyson's Punch Out.

As we grew older, sports began to make up a great part of our afterschool time. Outdoor activities and video games often took a backseat to baseball, soccer, football, swimming, and basketball practice. Sports were such a huge part of our lives throughout the year. Growing up in a rural area allowed my brothers and I to participate in many sports. Part of why I believe my childhood was so fulfilling was that there was a distinct balance between school and home. From the time the bus dropped us off until we hopped back on, the focus was on learning. Once home, however, time was relatively sacred when it came to play and spending quality time with family and friends.

The life of a child today has changed dramatically. Play, both in and out of school, has become a distant memory for many kids around the world. For reasons that make no sense to me, children are given obscene amounts of homework. Instead of coming home to unwind, play, and spend valuable time with family and friends, kids are stressed out beyond belief as high-stakes tests and homework have become the norm. Why have we veered off in this direction? There is little research to support the impact of homework on achievement for students in grades kindergarten through seven. When it is assigned it should be in small and meaningful amounts.

I am not in favor of abolishing homework entirely. As a child I was assigned homework, but it was a manageable amount that did not negatively impact social and play time. It was also not used in a high stakes way, such as determining a grade. As a parent, I want my children to reinforce at home what they have learned during the school day, but more importantly, I want them to be kids. During my tenure as principal, my district delved into the research with our students from all grade levels and changed our homework practices. Homework was still assigned, but there were time limits for each grade, and it could not be used to punish students academically.

Perhaps there will always be two sides to this debate. However, I think we must take a hard and objective look at the impact it is having on our kids. Current homework practices are making many students loathe school and learning. If your homework practices make kids dislike school and/or learning, that alone should tell you something must change.

I remember attending an event in my former community at which parents were lamenting how much homework their children had. I could relate because every night my wife and I battled with our kids over homework. My daughter cried and threw a fit. She sat in the car and did homework to and from cheer practice. That was her after school life in a nutshell. She completed homework for thirty-five minutes on the way to cheerleading practice. After 2-3 hours of cheer practice, she again worked on homework for another thirty-five minutes on the ride home. Sometimes she had even more work once she got home. My son just sat and stared back at us with an empty gaze. Ask any parent or child about their feelings on homework these days and you are bound to get a negative response.

If you currently work in a school consider this. Regardless of your views on homework, please take the time to reflect on whether it is actually having a positive impact on student learning and motivation. If homework is assigned, consider a balanced approach of meaningful assignments that reinforce thinking and learning in a timely fashion. It's time to address the elephant in the room (homework) if student learning and success are the ultimate goal.

## Reflective Conversations to Drive Thinking

Chapter 4 dove into the importance of scaffolding as a way to empower learners to engage in reflective thinking. It is also important for teachers and administrators to engage in opportunities or create the conditions to reflect. Most educators desire meaningful feedback that can be used as a catalyst for growth. When it comes to improving learning, criticism alone will rarely, if ever, lead to changes of professional practice. Here is the main difference between the two:

**Feedback** - information about reactions to a product, a person's performance, completion of a task, etc., used as a basis for improvement.

**Criticism** - the expression of disapproval of someone or something based on perceived faults or mistakes.

As you reflect on the two definitions above, which pathway would you prefer? Successful feedback lies in a variety of factors such as facilitation in a timely manner, detailing practical or specific strategies for improvement, ensuring the messaging is positive, consistently providing it, and at times choosing the right medium to convey the message. However, one of the most important considerations is to ensure that a two-way conversation takes place where there is a dialogue, not a monologue. Virtually no educator wants to have suggestions dictated to him or her.

A recent coaching visit at a school reminded me about the importance between the two. Over the course of a year, I had been working with the district on building pedagogical capacity both with and without technology. After visiting numerous classrooms, I met with a grade-level team and the administrators to facilitate a meaningful feedback conversation. Instead of just telling them what I saw and thought, I instead had them pair up and discuss their lessons using the following question prompts:

- How well do you think the lesson or activity went?
- What would you have done differently?

The point here was for them to begin to reflect on both the positive outcomes as well as the challenges they might have experienced. Lasting improvement comes from our own realizations as to what can be done to grow and improve rather than just being told how to grow and improve. After some volunteers shared how they thought their lesson went, I then challenged them with the following questions to facilitate a more in-depth analysis of the effectiveness of the lesson from their lens:

- How do you know your kids learned?
- Where was the level of thinking?
- How did students apply their thinking in relevant and meaningful ways?
- How did you push all kids regardless of where they were?
- What role did technology have in the process and who was the one using it?
- What accountability structures were put in place?
- How do you think your students perceived the lesson?

These questions prompted both the teachers and administrators in the room to think more critically about whether the lesson or activity achieved the desired outcome in relation to the aligned goal. My role during this time was simply to pose the questions and then actively listen. What was powerful from my seat was that I didn't even have to share most of the feedback I had written down because these educators offered it up themselves upon in-depth analysis of their lessons. This is not to say I didn't add more detail or provide specific strategies to improve, but the culture that was created through the use of the above questions was more empowering and designed to impart a sense of ownership among everyone present. Whether peer-to-peer or from a supervisory position, engage in a collaborative dialogue during any feedback conversation. Then provide time to process, further reflect, and develop action steps for improvement.

There are many factors that contribute to the creation of a disruptive thinking and learning culture both among students and adults. It is important to understand some of these phenomena in order to determine what typically fosters success. I often hear the phrase that we want our students to "think outside the box." For our students to think outside the box, we must first engage in outlier practices ourselves when it comes to many issues, including grading, homework, and feedback, as well as reflecting on our current practices and considering whether they are promoting—or inhibiting—disruptive thinking on the part of our students.

---

DISRUPTIVE CHALLENGE #7

Select an outlier practice where you see an opportunity for growth. Identify distinct changes, both mental and behavioral, that need to be made to improve practice in this area. To accomplish this consider engaging in the practice yourself. For example, complete the same homework that either you or a colleague assigns students for a week. Share your reflections and changes to practice on social media using the #DisruptiveThink hashtag.

# CHAPTER 8

# Sustaining a Culture of Disruptive Thinking

*"The most difficult thing is the decision to act, the rest is merely tenacity. The fears are paper tigers. You can do anything you decide to do."*

Ameila Earhart

As an identical twin, it was always a challenge going through school. Initially, my brother and I had to deal with the fact that our teachers could not tell us apart. My grandmother rectified this problem by outfitting each of us with belts that had our first initial on them. As we aged beyond the elementary years, teachers began to tell us apart better due to some slight differences in appearance that began to take shape as well as some major shifts in personality. Thank goodness for that, because we would never have survived the middle school years if we were still forced to wear those belts!

The second challenge came in the form of academic achievement. For my twin, learning and success, based on traditional metrics, came very easily. It seemed to me at least that he did not have to put in much effort to earn high marks on assessments. Obviously, my stance on grades and learning has changed a great deal since then, but this nonetheless posed yet another challenge of being a twin. I had to study twice as long or longer just to earn a B in many of the same classes where my brother got an A. School came much easier for him.

## Show You Care

My saving grace came in the form of some amazing teachers. I loved the life sciences, particularly biology. My love for science eventually led me to pursue an undergraduate degree in marine biology. This genuine interest took hold in the 7th grade thanks to Mr. South, my science teacher who I discussed in Chapter 4. As I entered high school I still had a strong interest in science, but struggled in certain courses such as chemistry and human anatomy. The struggle was amplified for me because my brother excelled in both courses.

Thankfully for me, Dr. Raymond Hynoski taught both these courses. He was a quirky fellow at times, but someone who had a firm grasp of the content and helped students master the concepts. Each of his classes was filled with humor, relevance, and inspiration that made everyone in the class feel as if they could become a chemist or doctor. His most endearing characteristic was how he consistently went above and beyond to let all students know that he cared. Each day I looked forward to attending his classes even if I struggled. I might not have done as well as I would have liked in his courses, but I tried hard and Dr. Hynoksi was able to emphasize even the slightest successes in my efforts to learn the concepts. I had to take chemistry. It was not a choice, but anatomy was an elective I signed up for only because Dr. Hynoski was the teacher.

There are many lessons that caring educators such as Dr. Hynoski teach us. So much pressure is placed on teachers and administrators to achieve at all costs. Rankings, stakeholder perceptions about the importance of standardized test scores, and honor rolls do nothing but make this issue more difficult. This is unfortunate because grades and scores are not what most students will remember later in life. What will resonate with students long after they have passed through our schools are the educators who believed in them. The ability of educators to provide hope and encouragement that inspire learners to follow their dreams and aspirations provides a priceless value that is not often acknowledged publicly, but greatly appreciated privately.

The power of empathy and the act of caring can mean the difference between a child dropping out of school or sticking it out through graduation. To some children, school serves as a refuge from the harsh world that is their unfortunate reality. It can also provide invaluable lessons that fuel a career path that otherwise might never have been imagined. Showing that we care on a daily basis only takes a little effort, but the potential payoff is much more valuable than what we could ever receive in a monetary sense.

All kids have greatness hidden inside them. It is the job of an educator to help them find and unleash that greatness. As adults, we must never forget the power of showing our students and each other that we care. Positive encouragement and support go a long way in helping others cope with the challenges of life while building lasting relationships. Take the time to mail a card, make a phone call, or send an electronic form of communication not just to those in need, but to others on a whim. There is no right or wrong way to nurture others, but we must be intentional about our caring acts. We often talk about the importance of showing instead of telling. Telling someone you care matters. But showing them you care with consistent, daily acts matters even more.

## Bring Out the Best in Kids

It's no secret that great cultures bring out the best in people, leading, in turn, to systemwide success. Success is a fickle thing, though. There might be specific indicators that are used to quantify whether an organization is good or even great, but there is no set recipe I know of for accomplishing this feat. What I do know is that it is not the result of one person or even one department. When systemic change happens and leads to widespread improved outcomes, it is always the result of the collective. One person, however, can be the catalyst for this type of change through a variety of strategies that empower the masses to become the very best they possibly can. As a reminder for myself in the work that I do, I created an acronym that outlines how to bring out the **BEST** in others:

- **Belief**
- **Empathy**
- **Selflessness**
- **Trust**

*Belief* is a superpower, in my opinion. Empowering others to believe not only in themselves, but also in something bigger than themselves, leads to innovative change and disruptive thinking and learning. Without it, the chances of implementing and sustaining change are next to zero. Belief in our learners also goes a long way to getting them to willingly engage in more challenging thinking and application of learning.

*Empathy* means, quite simply, showing others that you genuinely have compassion for what they are going through. It is vital for us to imagine ourselves in the position of our students. This gives us a better perspective on the challenges and feelings of those we are tasked to serve. Better, more informed decisions can result from "walking in the shoes" of those who will be most impacted by the choices we make. A culture of disruptive thinking and learning begins with a foundation of relationships built on trust and sustained through empathy.

*Selflessness* means putting others before yourself through both your words and your actions. It is about helping those around us or within our care and not looking for any recognition or something in return. The messages sent through selfless behaviors build people up in more ways than you will ever know. By selflessly serving others, a culture of respect and admiration will be created and will foster an attitude of disruptive thinking and learning. Even if you are in a position to hold others accountable, remember that you are just as accountable to them as they are to you. And, we are all accountable to the students we serve. Selfish behaviors, on the other hand, do everything but bring out the best in others. Most are not willing to give themselves up or work harder for someone who is unwilling to model selflessness themselves.

> Without trust, there is no relationship. If there is no relationship, no real learning or change will occur.
> _____

*Trust* might be the most critical element when it comes to bringing out the best in others. In the words of Brian Tacy (2010), "The glue that holds all relationships together—including the relationship between the leader and the led—is trust, and trust is based on integrity." Without trust, there is no relationship. If there is no relationship, no real learning or change will occur. In order to foster a culture of disruptive thinking and learning, we must first create cultures of safety, in which people feel "safe" to speak honestly, take risks, challenge the status quo, and be vulnerable. It is imperative to reflect on how we develop trust among the people with whom we work as well as the students and families we serve.

As you reflect on your role as an educator, think about how your actions bring out the **BEST** in others to get them to engage in disruptive thinking and learning.

## Unlock Potential

There are many elements to change. One of the most powerful is that of self-efficacy. Almost everyone can identify goals they want to accomplish or aspects about their personal and professional lives they would like to change. Here is where self-efficacy comes in. It plays a significant role in how goals, tasks, and challenges are approached and ultimately achieved. To improve one's future self, we must first reflect on our current reality. The next step is deciding where we eventually want to be. Finally, it is simply about initiating consistent, incremental action steps to close the gap from where we are today to where we ultimately wish to arrive. Success in this endeavor requires self-efficacy combined with a leap of faith.

For self-efficacy to play a role in the change process, we must always be open to improvement, holding ourselves accountable for ongoing advancement. This is why it is so important that we are our own most prominent critic and make reflection a daily part of our routine. No matter who you are and what you do, there are always opportunities to become better. The question is, will you pursue them?

Changing, growing, and improving is not about achieving perfection; that is not a reality in anyone's world. It is, however, about how we can become better each day, eventually becoming the best iteration of our unique selves. Our potential is often inhibited by a fixed mindset or an unwillingness to grow, as outlined in Chapter 2. We often perceive our talents and ideas as not being all that great. However, looking at where we put the most and least amount of time and effort into our practice, we can begin to unleash potential that we never thought was possible. It is OK to be unclear on any given day as to exactly where we want to be. In fact, it seems as if this is my daily reality. The key is never thinking that your current reality is "good enough."

If we want to help those we either serve or work with unlock their full potential, then we must first model the way. Think about where you are and where you eventually want to be. Apply the same lens to your classroom, school, organization, or district. Then take the leap of faith; trusting in your innate abilities to improve in ways you never thought possible. Will everything always work out the way you want it to? Sadly, no. Just remember that each journey, no matter the outcome, provides an invaluable learning experience. There is no better time than now to tap into your full potential.

## "What If?" Instead of "Yeah, But"

Imagine if everything went as planned in life. If this were the case, I am not sure that there would be any lengthy discussion about changing mindsets. As we are all acutely aware, even if you diligently take into account many potential variables, things still might not work out the way you planned. When this happens, it is not only frustrating, but it also impacts our psyche, resulting in an apprehension to try something new or different in the future. The saying, "what gets planned, gets done" still holds water to some extent. However, the outcome might impact your subsequent motivation to innovate to the point it is tempered or even drowned.

Planning aside, there is another inhibitory element lurking in every organizational culture, including education, and that is excuses. We all face challenges in the professional workplace such as not enough time, lack of funds, societal realities, limited support, too many initiatives or mandates, lack of collaboration, naysayers, and antagonists, to list a few. These are all legitimate challenges and we have to work even harder and more diligently to find workable solutions to overcome them, especially if the goal is to get all staff and students to practice disruptive thinking and learning. My concern arises when challenges that will always be present in some form or another eventually morph into excuses that hold us back from becoming our best selves.

At times we find ourselves in the midst of a crisis. Regardless of the situation it can only be used as an "excuse" for so long. Over time, these excuses evolve into patterns and habits that may hold us back forever if we fail to diligently and honestly address them. They are routinely used when our subconscious mind makes us feel that we are not smart, talented, or good enough to have what it is we want or deserve. This line of thinking begins the process in which we start viewing these external phenomena as excuses for why we can't do what we want to do.

If we continue to make excuses, it becomes a habit and even a way of living. This can prohibit us from developing potential in ourselves and others. To overcome this possible trap, we must either find or further expand our purpose as it relates to what we do. In the words of comedian Michael Junior (2017), "When you know your *why*, your *what* has more impact, because you are walking in or towards your purpose."

With a firm grasp on our purpose, it is easier to approach challenges with a "What if?" attitude instead of "Yeah, but" disposition. The former epitomizes a growth mindset and provides the needed motivation to move innovative change forward even if the desired outcome is not guaranteed. Think about how important this shift in thinking is when it comes to helping our learners find success. A "What if?" approach looks beyond any challenges to assist kids who need it the most. And, at times, every child we serve needs it the most. It also helps to unlock our potential and hidden talents.

Celebrate where you are and what you have accomplished, but never become complacent. The pursuit of arriving at your eventual destination begins by understanding there is no ultimate destination, except to keep pressing on and improving. Implementing and practicing disruptive thinking is a never-ending journey both for us and our students. We need to focus on the "What ifs?" instead of the "Yeah, buts" to help us on this journey.

## The Right Mindset

There are points in our professional lives that change us for the better. I vividly remember one such moment in 2009 when I took a device from a student who had it out in the hallway. Since this was a violation of school policy, I immediately confiscated the device, because this is what I thought I was supposed to do to ensure a school culture free from distraction and solely focused on traditional learning. I helped write the district policy blocking social media and at the school level made sure no mobile devices were seen or heard. As the student handed me his device to avoid a one day in-school suspension for open defiance, his message to me rocked my world—and not in a good way. He thanked me for creating a jail out of what should be a school. This was the moment in time that marked the beginning of my journey to becoming more of a disruptive thinker as a professional educator.

A mindset is an attitude, disposition, or mood with which a person approaches a situation. In short, it's a belief that determines the decisions we make, actions that are undertaken, and how situations are handled. How we think and act can help us identify opportunities for improvement. Mindsets can also function as a roadblock to progress. Our natural apprehension and fear associated with change inhibits our ability to pursue new ideas and implement them with fidelity. For sustainable change to take root and flourish there must be a belief that our actions can significantly improve outcomes. The best ideas come from those who constantly push their thinking as well as the thinking of others.

Mindsets go well beyond what a person thinks or feels. Gary Klein (2016) eloquently articulates what mindsets are and why they matter:

> "Mindsets aren't just any beliefs. They are beliefs that orient our reactions and tendencies. They serve a number of cognitive functions. They let us frame situations: they direct our attention to the most important cues, so that we're not overwhelmed with information. They suggest sensible goals so that we know what we should be trying to achieve. They prime us with reasonable courses of action so that we don't have to puzzle out what to do. When our mindsets become habitual, they define who we are, and who we can become" (para. 10).

Mindsets are not limited in scope and can be broken up into numerous subsets. The end goal of our work is to transform all facets of education to fundamentally improve thinking among all learners, both students and adults. The will and desire to change must be backed with action, accountability, and reflection. Doing things differently, jumping on the latest bandwagon, and claiming that some new way is a better way only matter if there is actual evidence of improvement.

## The Impact You Have

There's a story from years ago that tells of an elementary school teacher whose name was Mrs. Thompson. You may have heard it before, but it is never a bad idea to remind yourself of the impact that you have as an educator and this powerful message makes that impact clear every time I hear it:

As she stood in front of her fifth-grade class on the first day of school, she told her children a lie. Like most teachers, she looked at her students and told them that she loved them all the same. But that simply was not true, because there in the front row, slumped in his seat, was a little boy named Teddy Stoddard.

Mrs. Thompson had watched Teddy the year before and noticed that he didn't play well with the other children. His clothes were messy and he constantly needed a bath. Teddy could be unpleasant at times. It got to the point where Mrs. Thompson would take delight in marking his papers with a broad red pen and making bold X's and finally putting a Big "F" on the top of his papers.

At the school where Mrs. Thompson taught, she was required to review each child's past records. She put Teddy's off till last. When she finally reviewed his file, she was in for a surprise. Teddy's first-grade teacher wrote, "Teddy is a bright child with a ready laugh. He does his work neatly and has good manners. He's a joy to be around." His second-grade teacher wrote, "Teddy is an excellent student and well-liked by his classmates. But he's troubled because his mother has a terminal illness and life at home must be a struggle." His third-grade teacher wrote, "His mother's death has been hard on him. He tries to do his best but his father doesn't show much interest. His home life will soon affect him if steps aren't taken." Teddy's fourth-grade teacher wrote, "Teddy is withdrawn and doesn't show much interest in school. He doesn't have many friends and sometimes he even sleeps in class."

By now, Mrs. Thompson realized the problem and she was ashamed of herself. She felt even worse when her students brought her Christmas presents wrapped in beautiful ribbons and bright paper, except for Teddy's. His present was clumsily wrapped in heavy brown paper that he got from a grocery bag. Mrs. Thompson took pains to open it in the middle of the other presents. Some of the children started to laugh when she found a rhinestone bracelet with some of the stones missing and a bottle that was one-quarter full of perfume. But she stifled the children's laughter when she explained how pretty the bracelet was while putting it on and then dabbing some of the perfume on her wrist. Teddy Stoddard stayed after school that day just long enough to say,

"Mrs. Thompson, today you smell just like my mom used to." After the children left, she cried for at least an hour.

On this very day, she quit teaching reading, writing, and arithmetic and instead she began to teach children. Mrs. Thompson began to pay close attention to Teddy as she worked with him. As time went on, his mind seemed to come alive. The more she encouraged him, the faster he responded. By the end of the year, Teddy had become one of the smartest children in the class. Despite her lie, he had become one of her teacher's pets. A year later she found a note under the door from Teddy telling her that she was the best teacher he had ever had in his whole life.

Six years passed by and to her surprise, another note came from Teddy. He wrote that he had finished high school third in his class and that she was still the best teacher that he had ever had in his whole life. Four years later, another letter came, saying that while things had been tough at times, he stayed in school and stuck with it and that he had graduated from college with the highest of honors. He assured Mrs. Thompson that she was still the very best and favorite teacher he had ever had in his whole life.

Four more years passed by and yet another letter came. This time, he explained that after he got his bachelor's degree, he had decided to go a little further. Again, assuring her that she was still the best and favorite teacher he ever had. The letter was signed: Theodore F. Stoddard, MD.

The story doesn't end there. There was one final letter that spring. Teddy said that he had met this girl and that he was going to be married. He explained that his father had died a couple of years ago and he was wondering if Mrs. Thompson might agree to sit in the place, at his wedding, that was usually reserved for the mother of the groom. Of course, Mrs. Thompson did. She wore that bracelet, the one with the several rhinestones missing. She also made sure she was wearing the perfume that Teddy remembered his mother wearing on their last Christmas together. After the wedding, they hugged each other as Dr. Stoddard whispered in Mrs. Thompson's ear, "Thank you so much for making me feel important and showing me that I could make a difference."

Mrs. Thompson, with tears in her eyes, whispered back, "Teddy you have it all wrong. You were the one who taught me that I could make a difference. I didn't know how to teach until I met you."

The touching story, authored by Elizabeth Silance Ballard, appeared as a piece of fiction in *HomeLife Magazine* in 1974. It still speaks to us all in some form or another. Although you may have heard this story previously during your career in education, the lesson remains the same and is worth repeating. It provides an important reminder of your impact on kids now and in the future. As you read this fictional piece, your own "Teddy Stoddards" probably came to mind.

Never underestimate your vital role in impacting the life of a child. Students might not realize it now, but later in life many will thank you in their own way for your belief in and commitment to them. To fully prepare all learners for their future, we must create classrooms in which disruptive thinking is a major component of the learning process. Disruptive thinking in the classroom will only become a reality, however, when priceless relationships are in place. With these in place, your impact will be felt for generations as the learners you influence today disrupt the bold new world in ways that change it—and us—for the better.

# Resources

The premise of the book has been to disrupt our professional practice in order to disrupt our (and, more importantly, our students') thinking. To future-proof learning, we need to evaluate how we empower learners to think in more disruptive ways. Sprinkled throughout this book are resources that align to the content in specific chapters to help bring some needed clarity. I have included these links below. Since they are Google Docs, the content will be updated regularly. However, many educators want to know what this actually looks like in practice. With so some much emphasis these days on the *why*, the *how* and *what* usually are absent. *What* students and teachers do and *how* they do it still matters and we all get better when we share better ways of doing what we do to empower our learners to think disruptively.

While the book outlines the *how* in many cases I wanted to include artifacts of evidence from the field. In my work with schools around the world, I get to see firsthand innovative practices that challenge the status quo. Here you will see how concepts from the book combined with feedback I have provided has resulted in changes to practice. My hope is that these examples will help readers pave the way for disruptive thinking strategies in their classrooms or schools. This will be a work in progress and new examples will be added regularly, so please keep coming back.

Artifacts of Evidence (specific examples from classrooms and schools that align to strategies covered in the book) - **bit.ly/disruptartifacts**

Edtech Tools (Chapter 3 and 6) - **bit.ly/edtechdisrupt**

Station Rotation Template (Chapter 5) - **bit.ly/SRtemp**

Choice Board Templates (Chapter 5) - **bit.ly/CBtemplates**

# References

Adams-Blair H., Oliver G. (2011). Daily classroom movement: Physical activity integration into the classroom. International Journal of Health, Wellness, & Society, 1 (3), 147–154.

Anderson, L. W., & Krathwohl, D. R. (Eds.). (2001). A taxonomy for learning, teaching and assessing: A revision of Bloom's Taxonomy of educational objectives. Longman: New York.

Arrunda, W. (2015). Why failure is essential to success. Retrieved at www.forbes.com/sites/williamarruda/2015/05/14/why-failure-is-essential-to-success/?sh=67de08d17923

Bandura A. (1986). Social foundations of thought and action: A social cognitive theory. Englewood Cliffs, NJ: Prentice-Hall

Barrett, P., & Zhang, Y. (2009). Optimal learning spaces: Design implications for primary schools. Salford, UK: Design and Print Group.

Barrett, P., Zhang, Y., Davies, F., & Barrett, L. (2015). Clever classrooms: Summary findings of the HEAD Project (Holistic Evidence and Design). Salford, UK: University of Salford, Manchester.

Barrett, P., Zhang, Y., Moffat, J., & Kobbacy, K. (2013). A holistic, multi-level analysis identifying the impact of classroom design on pupils' learning.

Building and Environment, 59, 678–689.

Benner, M., Brown, C., & Jeffrey, A. (2019). Elevating student voice in education. Retrieved from www.americanprogress.org/issues/education-k-12/reports/2019/08/14/473197/elevating-student-voice-education/

Bosler, K. (2013). Make time for awe. Retrieved from www.theatlantic.com/health/archive/2013/12/make-time-for-awe/282245/

Braniff C. (2011). Perceptions of an active classroom: Exploration of movement and collaboration with fourth grade students. Networks: An On-line Journal for Teacher Research, 13 (1).

Bransford, J. D., Brown, A.L., & Cocking, R.R. (2000). *How People Learn: Brain, Mind, Experience and School.* National Academy Press: Washington D.C.

Briggs, S. (2014). How to make learning relevant to your students (and why it's crucial to their success). Retrieved from www.opencolleges.edu.au/informed/features/how-to-make-learning-relevant/

Browning C., Edson A.J., Kimani P., Aslan-Tutak F. (2014). Mathematical content knowledge for teaching elementary mathematics: A focus on geometry and measurement. Mathematics Enthusiast, 11 (2), 333–383.

Clark, R. C. & Mayer, R.E. (2008). Learning by Viewing Versus Learning by Doing: Evidence-Based Guidelines for Principled Learning Environments. *Performance Improvement*, 47(9)9, 5–13.

Comer, J. (1995). Lecture given at Education Service Center, Region IV. Houston, TX.

Costa, A. L., & Kallick, B. (2008). Learning and leading with habits of mind: 16 essential characteristics for success. Association for Supervision and Curriculum Development: Alexandria, VA

deWinstanley, P. & Bjork, R. (2002). Successful Lecturing: Presenting Information in Ways that Engage Effective Processing. New Directions for Teaching and Learning. 89, 19–31.

Dornhecker, M., Blake, J., Benden, M., Zhao, H., & Wendel, M. (2015). The effect of standbiased desks on academic engagement: An exploratory study. International Journal of Health Promotion and Education, 53(5), 271–280.

Dweck, C. S. (2006). Mindset: The new psychology of success. New York: Random House.

Erwin H., Fedewa A., Ahn S. (2013). Student academic performance outcomes of a classroom physical activity intervention: A pilot study. International Electronic Journal of Elementary Education, 5 (2), 109–124.

Fisher, A., Godwin, K., & Seltman, H. (2014). Visual environment, attention allocation, and learning in young children: When too much of a good thing may be bad. Psychological Science, 25(7), 1362–1370.

Fleming, L. (2017). The Kickstart Guide to Making GREAT Makerspaces. Corwin: Thousand Oaks, CA.

Finley, T. (2013). Rethinking whole class discussion. Retrieved from www.edutopia.org/blog/rethinking-whole-class-discussion-todd-finley

Ford, H. (1922). My Life and Work. Binker North.

Ford, K. N. (2016). The impact of physical movement on academic learning. Culminating Projects in Teacher Development, 13.

Freeman, S., Eddy, S.L., McDonough, M., Smith, M.K, Okoroafor, N., Jordt, H., & Wenderoth, M.P. (2004). Active learning increases student performance in science, engineering, and mathematics. *Proceedings of the National Academy of Sciences of the United States of America, 111*(23), 8410-8415.

Ganske, K. (2017). Lesson Closure: An important piece of the student learning puzzle. *The Reading Teacher. 70*(1), 100.

Garner, B. (2017). Fear Has Two Meanings – Which Will You Choose. Retrieved from www.bobgarneronline.com/blog/

Gerstein, J. (2015). All kids have worth. Retrieved from usergeneratededucation.wordpress.com/2015/02/27/all-kids-have-worth/

Ginsburg, K. R. (2007). The importance of play in promoting healthy child development and maintaining strong parent-child bonds. *Pediatrics* 119, 182–191.

Goodwin, B., & Miller, K. (2012). Good Feedback Is Targeted, Specific, Timely. *Educational Leadership, 70*(1), 82-83.

Guskey, T. R. (2000). Grading policies that work against standards ... and how to fix them. NASSP Bulletin, 84(620), 20–29.

Halpern, D. F. & Hakel, M.D. (2003) Applying the Science of Learning. *Change: The Magazine of Higher Learning, 35*(4), 36–41.

Hattie, J. (2008). Visible Learning. Routledge: Boca Raton, FL.

Hatton, N., & Smith, D. (1995). Reflection in teacher education: Towards definition and implementation. *Teaching and Teacher Education, 11*(1), 33–49.

Henderson, P., & Karr-Kidwell, P. J. (1998). Authentic assessment: An extensive literary review and recommendations for administrators. Retrieved from ERIC Database ED41840.

Hughes, J. (Producer and Director). (1986). *Ferris Bueller's Day Off* [Motion Picture]. United States: Paramount Pictures

Hunter, M. (1967). Teach More–Faster! TIP Publications: El Segundo, CA

Junior, Michael (2017). Know your why. Retrieved from www.youtube.com/watch?v=1ytFB8TrkTo&ab_channel=MichaelJr.

Junkala, J. (2018). Comfort is the enemy of progress. Retrieved from medium.com/@joanijunkala/comfort-is-the-enemy-of-progress-3c861f758a6f

Klein, G. (2016). Mindsets: What they are and why they matter. Retrieved from hwww.psychologytoday.com/us/blog/seeing-what-others-dont/201605/mindsets.

Kohn, A. (2011). The case against grades. Educational Leadership, 69(3), 28–33.

Lenz, M. (2016). 3 categories of beliefs, and why separating them is important. Retrieved from www.biblicalleadership.com/blogs/3-categories-of-beliefs-and-why-separating-them-is-important/

Lew, M. & Schmidt, H. (2011). Self-reflection and academic performance: Is there a relationship? *Advances in Health Sciences Education: Theory and Practice.* 16, 529-45.

Martinuzzi, B. (2009). The Leader as a Mensch: Become the Kind of Person Others Want to Follow. Freedom, CA: Six Seconds.

Mayer, R. E. (2011). Applying the science of learning. New York, NY: Pearson.

McDermott, K. B., Agarwal, P.K, D'Antonio, L., Roediger III, H.L, & McDaniel, M.A. (2014). Both multiple-choice and short-answer quizzes enhance later exam performance in middle and high school classes. *Journal of Experimental Psychology: Applied,* 20 (1), 3-21.

McTighe, J. (2015). What is a Performance Task? (Part 1). Retrieved from blog.performancetask.com/what-is-a-performance-task-part-1-9fa0d99ead3b

Nicol, D. (2010). From monologue to dialogue: improving written feedback processes in mass higher education. Assessment & Evaluation in Higher Education,

35(5), 501-517.

O'Connor, K. (2007). A repair kit for grading: 15 fixes for broken grades. Portland, OR: Educational Testing Service.

O'Connor, K., & Wormeli, R. (2011). Reporting student learning. Educational Leadership, 69(3), 40-44.

Reeves, D. B. (2004). The case against zero. Phi Delta Kappan, 86(4), 324–325.

Reeves, D. B. (2008). Effective grading practices. Educational Leadership, 65(5), 85–87.

Revington, S. (2016). Defining authentic learning. Retrieved from authenticlearning.weebly.com/

Rose, E. J., Sierschynski, J., & Björling, E. A. (2016). Reflecting on reflections: Using video in learning reflection to enhance authenticity. Journal of Interactive Technology & Pedagogy, 9. Retrieved from https://jitp.commons.gc.cuny.edu/reflecting-on-reflections-using-video-in-learning-reflection-to-enhance-authenticity/

Sattelmair, J., & Ratey, J. J. (2009). Physically active play and cognition. American Journal of Play, 3, 365–374.

Scott-Webber, L., Strickland, A., & Kapitula, L. (2014). How classroom design affects student engagement. Steelcase Education.

Sheninger, E. (2019). Digital Leadership: Changing Paradigms for Changing Times (2nd Edition). Corwin: Thousand Oaks, CA.

Sheninger, E. (2015). Uncommon Learning. Corwin: Thousand Oaks, CA

Sheninger E. & Murray, T. (2017). Learning Transformed: 8 Keys to Designing Tomorrow's Schools, Today. ASCD: Alexandria, VA.

Sinek, S. (2009). How great leaders inspire action. Retrieved from www.ted.com/talks/simon_sinek_how_great_leaders_inspire_action

Smith, M. K., Wood, W. B., Adams, W. K., Wieman, C., Knight, J. K., Guild, N. & Su, T. T. (2009) Why peer discussion improves student performance on in-class concept questions. Science 323 (5910):122–24.

Spiro, R.J. & Jehng, J. (1990). Cognitive flexibility and hypertext: Theory and technology for the non-linear and multidimensional traversal of complex subject matter. In D. Nix & R. Spiro (eds.), *Cognition, Education, and Multimedia*. Hillsdale, NJ: Erlbaum.

Stockard, Jean & W. Wood, Timothy & Coughlin, Cristy & Rasplica Khoury, Caitlin. (2018). The Effectiveness of Direct Instruction Curricula: A Meta-Analysis of a Half Century of Research. *Review of Educational Research*: 88(4).

Tomlinson, C. (2016). The Differentiated Classroom: Responding to the Needs of All Learners (2nd Edition). Association for Supervision and Curriculum Development: Alexandria, VA.

Tracey, B. (2010). How the Best Leaders Lead. AMACOM.

Trambley, E. (2017). Breaks in the elementary classroom and their effect on student behavior. Capstone Projects and Master's Thesis, California State University, Monterey Bay.

Vazou, S., Gavrilou, P., Mamalaki, E., Papanastasiou, A., & Sioumala, N. (2012). Does integrating physical activity in the elementary school classroom influence academic motivation? *International Journal of Sport & Exercise Psychology*, 10(4), 251–263.

Voltz, D.L., & Damiano-Lantz, M. (1993, Summer). Developing ownership in learning. Teaching Exceptional Children, 18-22.

Wiggins, G., & McTighe, J. (2004). Understanding by Design Professional Development Workbook. Association for Supervision and Curriculum Development: Alexandria, VA.

William, D. (2011). Embedded formative assessment. Solution Tree Press: Bloomington, IN.

Wormeli, R. (2006). Fair isn't always equal: Assessing and grading in a differentiated classroom. Portland ME: Stenhouse Publishers.

# Acknowledgements

True innovation in education happens when educators, schools, and districts take ideas and implement them in ways that lead to positive changes and outcomes. Throughout this book I referenced numerous coaching experiences to help add context and strengthen the points I was trying to make. I can honestly say that this manuscript would never have materialized had it not been for the amazing educators I have been blessed to work with in long-term projects on an ongoing basis. Thank you to the teachers and administrators in the following schools and districts who have not only shaped my thinking but also shown me what is possible in education when collective action is taken to create a culture that supports disruptive thinking:

Corinth School District (Corinth, MS)
Davis School District (Farmington, UT)
Elmhurst School District 205 (Elmhurst, IL)
Howell Elementary STEM School (Columbia, TN)
Ida Redmond Taylor Elementary School (Santa Maria, CA)
Juab School District (Nephi, UT)
Mount Olive School District (Flanders, NJ)
Paterson Public Schools (Paterson, NJ)
Weehawken Township School District (Weehawken, NJ)
Wells Elementary School (Cypress, TX)

Each example in the book, whether direct or subtle, materialized from the schools and districts listed above. Although my job was to support these educators, in doing so, I learned so much from them in ways that continue to both influence and empower me in my work.

# About the Author

E ric Sheninger is an Associate Partner with the *International Center for Leadership in Education* (ICLE). Prior to this, he was the award-winning principal at New Milford High School. Under his leadership his school became a globally recognized model for innovative practices. Eric oversaw the successful implementation of several sustainable change initiatives that radically transformed the learning culture at his school while increasing achievement.

His work focuses on empowering educators to unlock the potential in all learners as well as themselves. Eric has emerged as an innovative leader, best-selling author, and sought-after speaker. Eric has received numerous awards and acknowledgments for his work. He is a Center for Digital Education Top 30 Award recipient, Bammy Award winner, National Association for Secondary School Principals Digital Principal Award winner, Phi Delta Kappa Emerging Leader Award recipient, winner of Learning Forward's Excellence in Professional Practice Award, Google Certified Innovator, Adobe Education Leader, and Association for Supervision and Curriculum Development 2011 Conference Scholar. He has authored or coauthored seven books, including best-sellers *Digital Leadership: Changing Paradigms for Changing Times*, *Uncommon Learning: Creating Schools That Work for Kids*, and *Learning Transformed: 8 Keys for Designing Tomorrow's School's, Today*.

Eric began his career in education as a science teacher at Watchung Hills Regional High School in Warren, New Jersey. He then transitioned into the field of educational administration, first as an athletic director and supervisor of physical education and health and then as vice principal in the New Milford School District. During his administrative career, he has served as district affirmative action officer and is the current president of the New Milford Administrators' Association.

Eric earned a Bachelor of Science degree from Salisbury University, a Bachelor of Science from the University of Maryland Eastern Shore, and a Master of Education in educational administration from East Stroudsburg University. To learn more about Eric's work, visit ericsheninger.com, or follow @E_Sheninger on Twitter.

# More from
# ConnectEDD Publishing

Since 2015, ConnectEDD has worked to transform education by empowering educators to become better-equipped to teach, learn, and lead. What started as a small company designed to provide professional learning events for educators has grown to include a variety of services to help teachers and administrators address essential challenges. ConnectEDD offers instructional and leadership coaching, professional development workshops focusing on a variety of educational topics, a roster of nationally recognized educator associates who possess hands-on knowledge and experience, educational conferences custom-designed to meet the specific needs of schools, districts, and state/national organizations, and ongoing, personalized support, both virtually and onsite. In 2020, ConnectEDD expanded to include publishing services designed to provide busy educators with books and resources consisting of practical information on a wide variety of teaching, learning, and leadership topics. Please visit us online at *connecteddpublishing.com* or contact us at: *info@connecteddpublishing.com*

**Recent Publications:**

*Live Your Excellence: Action Guide* by Jimmy Casas
*Culturize: Action Guide* by Jimmy Casas
*Daily Inspiration for Educators: Positive Thoughts for Every Day of the Year* by Jimmy Casas

*Eyes on Culture: Multiply Excellence in Your School* by Emily Paschall

*Pause. Breathe. Flourish. Living Your Best Life as an Educator* by William D. Parker

*L.E.A.R.N.E.R. Finding the True, Good, and Beautiful in Education* by Marita Diffenbaugh

*Educator Reflection Tips Volume II: Refining Our Practice* by Jami Fowler-White

*Handle With Care: Managing Difficult Situations in Schools with Dignity and Respect* by Jimmy Casas and Joy Kelly